Faith Diving

A Progressive Lutheran Confirmation Curriculum

By Pastor Adrian Bonaro

Faith Diving 3 Year Schedule

Year 1

Day 1 Why We Do What We Do	1
Day 2 Unbelief	5
Day 3 Creation and Evolution	9
Day 4 Meet With a Naturalist	16
Day 5 Oddities of the World Explored	18
Day 6 Ghosts	22
Day 7 Old Testament Overview	26
Day 8 Old Testament Interactive	29
Day 9 Genesis to Exodus Mystery Science	32
Day 10 10 commandments Scavenger Hunt	36
Day 11 Other Old Testament Books	45
Day 12 Judaism/Synagogue	48
Day 13 Hot Button	51
Day 14 Big Question Day	53
Day 15 Faith Diver Graduation	56
Day 16 Movie for Continuing Students	57

Year 2

Day 17 Christianity Overview	58
Day 18 New Testament Overview	63
Day 19 Jesus and the Gospels	66
Day 20 Acts and Faith healings	71
Day 21 Other New Testament Books	76
Day 22 Christianity vs. Not Christianity Debate	82
Day 23 Apostle's Creed/Why Christianity	85
Day 24 Lord's Prayer Scavenger Hunt	88
Day 25 History of Christianity	94
Day 26 Attend a Non-Lutheran Service	103
Day 27 Plan and Lead Perfect Christian Event	104
Day 28 Outreach Plan	107
Day 29 Hot Button	108
Day 30 Big Question Day	110
Day 31 Faith Diver Graduation	113
Day 32 Movie for Continuing Students	114

Year 3

Day 33 Lutheran?/Luther Video Part 1	115
Day 34 Luther Video Part 2/95 Theses	121
Day 35 Meet Bishop	125
Day 36 Luther's Dark Side/American Lutheranism	127
Day 37 Talk to other Lutherans/Service Project	131
Day 38 Figuring out Your Calling/Vocation	133
Day 39 Create Your Own Mission Start	136
Day 40 Different Parts of a Worship Service	138
Day 41 Plan A Sunday Worship Service	141
Day 42 Lead Worship Service	143
Day 43 World Religions Part 1	144
Day 44 World Religions Part 2	147
Day 45 What do You Believe?	149
Day 46 Hot Button	152
Day 47 Big Question	154
Day 48 Faith Diver Graduation	157

Faith Diving Introduction

I have often wondered about the purpose of "confirmation." Not the ritual of confirmation itself, but the confirmation classes. An important part of our Lutheran tradition is the ritual "Affirmation of Baptism" or confirmation where we claim hold of the promises that were made in our Baptism and say before others, "Yes, this is me. I claim this faith as my own. I'm thankful that God chose me in my Baptism and now I choose God in return." That is truly an important ritual, but confirmation classes? I have never fully understood how they are supposed to function.

We cram a bunch of information into a youth's brain, hoping it will somehow stick. Even though we know it won't. We don't necessarily give them real opportunities to question, instead telling them, "This is how it is." And then we watch, as shortly after confirmation, the youth disappears from the church. I can't speak for every youth, but I know why I initially thought about leaving the church after my confirmation. I met something in my faith life for which confirmation did not prepare me. Like many others, I faced a challenge, a question, a hard piece of life, and I made the decision to leave faith behind (temporarily in my case) as childish.

I have always wanted to find a way to help youth avoid some of the hard, doubt filled, angst ridden moments that I went through as I worked, and God worked, to get my faith where it needed to be. My thinking on confirmation has always been, what if we put the challenges, the questions, the hard to answer situations in front of our youth as they go through confirmation classes? What if we brought to the surface the real struggles they are going to face in their faith life while they are in a safe environment, while they are still in a place where they are willing to hear "church" answers?

This curriculum that you hold in your hand, that I call Faith Diving, is my attempt to provide what I think youth actually need in order to weather the storm that will come post confirmation, post childlike faith.

It is a three year curriculum, but not everyone has time for a three year curriculum. It features 16 class sessions per year, but not everyone has time for 16 class sessions while also managing sports and holidays and trips and whatever else might come the youth's way in this ever busy world. It is meant to take the youth from conversations about God in general, to conversations about God in Christianity, to conversations about God in Lutheranism and other religions. How you get the youth through this schedule and how much of each day you actually use is completely up to you. And to be honest, most days have too much material for a single class.

This confirmation curriculum is built to challenge the youth. It is built to make them ask questions. It is built to somewhat address the parts of our faith we don't always get into. Just as diving from up high can be scary, so too can be faith diving. But with a loving leader to guide them through the process, even the most terrifying waters can become a grand adventure. Through the use of games, experiential events, multimedia, and nearly every other possible interactive element this curriculum seeks to teach all the "standard" pieces of confirmation while giving the youth every opportunity to gain the answers they need to face this truly complicated world that we live in.

This curriculum is not perfect. I have taught all the way through it three times now, which adds up to nine years of trial and error. Each year I change the curriculum. I add. I rewrite. I delete. I reimagine. I hope as you work to educate your youth during this most important time, that you will do the same. Find what works for your youth. Find what doesn't. Let me know how it goes.

I have one goal in all of this and it isn't financial profit. It is to help youth bypass times of faith crisis, times of crushing doubt, and feelings of purposelessness to reach the other side where the reality of God, the fullness of God, the companionship of God is before their eyes at every moment.

Now, let me leave you with one last thought. When I was a student at the University of Washington, I did an independent study with a former Presbyterian minister turned college professor. We were talking about the youth group I was leading and how I didn't know what activity I was going to do with them that week. His answer, without pause, without me actually asking a question was, "Love them. Just love them. That is all you ever need to do. Let them know they are loved."

At the time I thought it was wildly impractical advice. If kids showed up to youth group expecting an exciting activity and all I did was let them know how much I loved them, I doubted that they would be back for another event. But in truth his advice couldn't have been any more practical. The kids in my youth group didn't come back each week because I had the most exciting games or gave the most interesting lessons, they came back (and they eventually told me so) because they knew that I cared about them.

Leading a confirmation class is not always easy. In fact, there are days when it is not really enjoyable. But on those days when the curriculum doesn't seem to be working and the lessons are not getting through, I invite you to strive first and foremost to love the youth in your class. So many times it is that love, that connection, that can draw people back to faith when they've lost their way. Love should always be the priority of any class time with youth (and adults for that matter).

Blessings on you as you take on this most important, most necessary, most vital mission.

Pastor Adrian Bonaro
ELCA Pastor

Year 1
God in General and Old Testament

Faith Diving Day 1
Getting to know the church
Location: Inside Sanctuary

Opening Prayer
Before you pray, ask they youth:

> Why do we pray?
> Is there a wrong way to pray?
> Do you pray? If so, why? If not, why not?

Then pray a repeat after me prayer.

Highs/Lows
Have the youth share a high event (good) and a low event (bad) from the last week.

Ice breaker game
Have them pair off and create a list of everything "religious" that they can find in the church sanctuary and what that is used for or why it is important.

Get to know the church
Have the youth that has the most "religious items" read off their list and then as they go through the list, explain what each of the items they listed actually mean and its history. See some examples below:

The Baptismal Font
Have water present in a pitcher, pour the water into the font, run your hands through the water. Invite them to stand around it and run their hands through it. Ask them:

> What is this for?
> What do we do with it?
> What does a baptism ritual look like?

Take them through the Baptismal rite as it occurs at your congregation. Ask them:

> But why do we do baptism?
> What is gained from it?
> Is it necessary for salvation?

Remind them that being baptized is like putting on a cloak of Christ (if you have a robe nearby, use it to give a very visual demonstration). Remind them that all the bad things they are doing are forgotten because when God looks at you, God sees Jesus (the robe), instead of the bad.

Remembrance of baptism reminds us how much we are protected and cared for. It does not suddenly make you a sinless person who never doubts, or fears, or makes mistakes. It is simply a marker, a claiming, you are completely and truly a child of God now and that adoption is for life. Baptism is not about exclusion, saying that those who don't have it are outside of God's love, it is instead about saying that these specific people that have received this baptist have explicitly and clearly been marked for God.

The Altar
Have communion elements present. Walk them through how communion is done at your congregation. Allow them to eat the bread and drink the wine directly from the altar. Explain to them why communion is important to you. Ask them:

> Why is communion important to you?
> Is it important?
> What do you think is gained out of it?

Talk about the candles and the significance of lighting those candles.

Talk about offering plates, what it means to tithe and offer a portion of what we have up to God.

Lectern
Have a Bible present on the Lectern. Explain why the Bible is important to you. Ask them:

> What do you think about the Bible?
> Is the Bible important?
> Why should people read it?

Cross
Give them a second to look up at the cross in front of the church. Ask them:

> What does the cross mean to you?

Pews
Ask them what is special about the pews? They probably won't offer up much, but tell them about the "priesthood of all believers" (that we are all able to connect directly with God, not just the pastor, and we are all given a calling to spread God's message through our unique individual gifts).

Blessing
Have them bless one another... have them mark the sign of the cross on their neighbor's forehead or hand and then say something nice that they hope will happen to them. After they bless each other, talk about how they did a very "priestly" action.

Play an around the church game
Sardines: This is somewhat of a reverse hide and seek game. The "it" person is sent out to hide. After about a minute, send out the rest of the youth to search for the "it" person. And instead of tagging the person or switching who is "it" the people that find the "it" person

hide with that person. The game goes on until every single youth has hid alongside the "it" person. The first person to find the "it" person is now the "it" person as you restart the game.

Close in Prayer

Homework
Answer:
Why do you think some people don't believe in God?

Faith Diving Day 2
Unbelief
Location: Somewhere with a fire pit

Begin inside... preferably where there is a white board.

Opening Prayer
Say something off the top of your head or something like: Gracious and loving God we come to you today with the knowledge that many people feel alone in this world. They don't know that you are looking out for them and caring for them. Please allow your loving presence and comfort to enter into their lives. In your holy name we pray. Amen.

Highs/Lows
Have the youth share a high event (good) and a low event (bad) from the last week.

Going Over The Homework
Ask the youth to get out their homework assignments. Ask them to offer up their ideas for why people don't believe in God. Make as thorough notes of their ideas as possible (writing them on a big board if one is available).

Give them as much time to discuss as they want. Be patient with them. If they get stalled, offer up some ideas:

> Theodicy (problem of evil and suffering in the world)
> Evolution explains God away
> Parts of the Bible untrue, so it is all untrue
> If God sends people to hell then I don't believe in God
> Evils in Church history
> They were never part of a religion
> It is only a matter of time until we understand all
> The evil thrive and the good die young
> God wouldn't work how any religions say God works
> Religion only exists to make people feel better.

When discussion has reached a good transition point, lead the youth to the fire pit.

Fire Pit Discussion
Sit kids in a circle around the fire pit. Make sure they stay silent as they take time to watch the fire. Ask them:

> What do you think people early on in creation thought when they saw fire?
> What did they think when they saw a Volcano erupt or when lightning struck the ground?
> How do you think the first people of a religion came to their religion?

Now you are going to want to familiarize yourself with the below information ahead of time, as you will work to give a speech/tell a story about the natural world. Explain that many early religions would identify the Gods with elements in nature, like a volcano, or the sun or the trees. Many early rituals even involved fire like the one you are sitting around. In nearly every major religion, fire is featured in it. It inspires fear or makes people understand true power.

What Fire Is
Many would say those that believe God is present in fire don't understand fire like we do now. We know that this fire is, "a chemical reaction that converts a fuel and oxygen into carbon dioxide and water."[1] It is not God in the smoke drifting back up to the heavens, it is, "made up of small particles, gases and water vapor. Water vapor makes up the majority of smoke. The remainder includes carbon monoxide, carbon dioxide, nitrogen oxide, irritant volatile organic compounds, air toxics and very small particles."[2]

---

[1] https://www.newscientist.com/question/what-is-fire/

[2] https://www.fs.usda.gov/Internet/FSE_DOCUMENTS/stelprdb5318238.pdf

Where we thought there was magic, we have found order. But at times, the order of the world remains impossible for us to understand. Ask them:

> Does understanding how something works mean God is not a part of that thing?
> Does knowing what smoke/fire is make it so we can't use it to connect with God? (Like using a candle/incense)

What Water is

Give out cocoa to the kids around the fire. As they enjoy their cocoa, pour some of yours on the water, watch the fire crackle. Explain that water is the source of our lives, we need it, it refreshes us, it sustains us. For a long time it was not understood what water was clean and what water would make people sick. So it was supposed that God ordained clean water and contaminated water. Now we know about microorganisms and disease, but our fascination with water has not ended.

For almost all substances the solid form is heavier than the liquid. But not for water. Ice floats. This allows for the survival of fish in the winter, but also ice skating. Imagine how impossible things would be if water did not behave in this unexpected way. We have come to understand more about the world, but that the world should work out the way that it does remains mysterious to even the most learned individual. Ask them:

> Is there anything that really amazes you about the world?
> Is there something that you don't understand and seems like magic?

Magically in the Right Place

For one example of our amazing natural world let them know that the earth has to be exactly as it is for us to be able to live on it. We can handle, for the most part, the coldest and the hottest of temperatures, (put your hand a comfortable position away from the fire) but if the earth were just a little bit further away from the sun, it would be colder... too cold (pull your hand away from the fire). Or if the earth were just a little closer (put your hand too close to the fire) it would be hotter, too hot.

What is the point of all of this? To many, the world seems to have some unexplainable order and for some, this is enough to make them believe that something more is out there, just like that old volcano that made people believe in a God. Ask them:

> Can you think of anything in creation/the world that makes you believe in God?

Special Guest
Have a member of the church at the fire pit to talk to the youth about how they went from unbelief to faith.

If Have Time
Come back inside (or stay around the campfire) and ask the youth to share why they believe in God (and let them be honest if they don't believe in God). Also share your faith story with them (why you believe).

Close in Prayer

Homework
Answer:
How do you think the world was made?
Does Evolution work with what you believe or against it?

Faith Diving Day 3
Creation and Evolution
Location: Inside

Opening Prayer
Begin with a word of Prayer on the glory of God's creation.

Highs/Lows
Have the youth share a high event (good) and a low event (bad) from the last week.

Going Over The Homework
Ask the youth to get out their homework assignments. Ask them:

> How do you think the world was made?
> Does Evolution work with what you believe?

What is Evolution?
Ask the youth to define evolution. A simple statement about evolution in biology would be that "the various types of plants, animals, and other living things on Earth have their origin in other preexisting types and that the distinguishable differences are due to modifications in successive generations."[3]

Evolution Game
This is an old, simple game, so I can't cite its exact origins, but all you need is two pieces of paper per youth, and a box of paperclips. Give each "Faith Diver" a piece of paper. Explain to them that they will need that piece of paper to reach a box of paperclips that will be about eight feet away from them. They can fold/crumple/alter their piece of paper however they want without "adding anything" to it.

---

[3] https://www.britannica.com/science/evolution-scientific-theory

After they have their paper ready, set them up behind a line that they cannot cross. They cannot modify their paper during this first round. Place the box about eight feet from them. Set a timer for two minutes. Allow the youth to try to touch the box as many times as they can within the two minutes (After they fling their paper at the box they can go retrieve it, without getting in anyone's way). If they manage to hit the paperclip box, have them take a paperclip to keep track of their successes.

Now explain to the youth that those paperclips were like food, and their papers were like early organisms on the hunt for food. Depending on how strict you want to be, those that got no paperclips would not get to go to the second round, but grace is always an important lesson too. For this second round give them a new piece of paper and have them modify it once again. All paperclips should be returned to the paperclip box. Set your timer once again and let chaos commence.

Once the game is finished, ask the youth if the game reminds them of anything. Explain that the game is like evolution, where generation after generation fights for food (paperclips) and each generation is improved (more or less) as they more effectively reproduce and gather needed resources. Have the youth line up their papers and show the differences and explain how the diversity of their papers mirrors the diversity we see in creatures throughout the world.

Evolution Discussion
Gather the youth around a table and ask them:

> Do you find evolution conflicts with your faith?
>> Why or why not?
> How many creation accounts are there in Genesis?
> Do you know if the two creation accounts agree with each other?

Group Play Acting
Break into two groups (One for Genesis 1, One for Genesis 2) and have the youth act out a creation account without words (charades) with the other side interpreting those actions. After each section have someone that is part of the group explain what was actually happening with their acting.

Prize (SNACKS) go to best acting and presentation.

Scripture

Genesis Chapter 1 NRSV (Slightly Edited)
In the beginning when God created the heavens and the earth, the earth was a formless void and darkness covered the face of the deep, while a wind from God swept over the face of the waters. Then God said, "Let there be light"; and there was light. And God saw that the light was good; and God separated the light from the darkness. God called the light Day, and the darkness he called Night. And there was evening and there was morning, the first day.

And God said, "Let there be a dome in the midst of the waters, and let it separate the waters from the waters." So God made the dome and separated the waters that were under the dome from the waters that were above the dome. And it was so. God called the dome Sky. And there was evening and there was morning, the second day.

And God said, "Let the waters under the sky be gathered together into one place, and let the dry land appear." And it was so. God called the dry land Earth, and the waters that were gathered together he called Seas. And God saw that it was good. Then God said, "Let the earth put forth vegetation:plants yielding seed, and fruit trees of every kind on earth that bear fruit with the seed in it." And it was so. The earth brought forth vegetation:plants yielding seed of every kind, and trees of every kind bearing fruit with the seed in it. And God saw that it was good. And there was evening and there was morning, the third day.

And God said, "Let there be lights in the dome of the sky to separate the day from the night; and let them be for signs and for seasons and for days and years, and let them be lights in the dome of the sky to give light upon the earth." And it was so. God made the two great lights—the greater light to rule the day and the lesser light to rule the night—and the stars. God set them in the dome of the sky to give light upon the earth, to rule over the day and over the night, and to separate the light from the darkness. And God saw that it was good. And there was evening and there was morning, the fourth day.

And God said, "Let the waters bring forth swarms of living creatures, and let birds fly above the earth across the dome of the sky." So God created the great sea monsters and every living creature that moves, of every kind, with which the waters swarm, and every winged bird of every kind. And God saw that it was good. God blessed them, saying, "Be fruitful and multiply and fill the waters in the seas, and let birds multiply on the earth." And there was evening and there was morning, the fifth day.

And God said, "Let the earth bring forth living creatures of every kind:cattle and creeping things and wild animals of the earth of every kind." And it was so. God made the wild animals of the earth of every kind, and the cattle of every kind, and everything that creeps upon the ground of every kind. And God saw that it was good.

Then God said, "Let us make humankind in our image, according to our likeness; and let them have dominion over the fish of the sea, and over the birds of the air, and over the cattle, and over all the wild animals of the earth, and over every creeping thing that creeps upon the earth."

So God created humankind in his image, in the image of God he created them; male and female he created them. God blessed them, and God said to them, "Be fruitful and multiply, and fill the earth and subdue it; and have dominion over the fish of the sea and over the birds of the air and over every living thing that moves upon the earth." God said, "See, I have given you every plant yielding seed that is upon the face of all the earth, and every tree with seed in its fruit; you shall have them for food. And to every beast of the earth, and to every bird of the air, and to everything that creeps on the earth, everything that has the breath of life, I have given every green plant for food." And it was so. God saw everything that he had made, and indeed, it was very good. And there was evening and there was morning, the sixth day.

Genesis 2 NRSV (Slightly Edited)
In the day that the Lord God made the earth and the heavens, when no plant of the field was yet in the earth and no herb of the field had yet sprung up—for the Lord God had not caused it to rain upon the earth, and there was no one to till the ground; but a stream would rise from the earth, and water the whole face of the ground—then the Lord God formed man from the dust of the ground, and breathed into his nostrils the breath of life; and the man became a living being. And the Lord God planted a garden in Eden, in the east; and there he put the man whom he had formed. Out of the ground the Lord God made to grow every tree that is pleasant to the sight and good for food, the tree of life also in the midst of the garden, and the tree of the knowledge of good and evil.

Then the Lord God said, "It is not good that the man should be alone; I will make him a helper as his partner." So out of the ground the Lord God formed every animal of the field and every bird of the air, and brought them to the man to see what he would call them; and whatever the man called every living creature, that was its name. The man gave names to all cattle, and to the birds of the air, and to every animal of the field; but for the man there was not found a helper as his partner. So the Lord God caused a deep sleep to fall upon the man, and he slept; then he took one of his ribs and closed up its place with flesh. And the rib that the Lord God had taken from the man he made into a woman and brought her to the man. Then the man said, "This at last is bone of my bones and flesh of my flesh; this one shall be called Woman, for out of Man this one was taken."

Creation Accounts Discussion

Gathering the youth back in a room with a whiteboard, ask them:

> Do the two accounts agree?
> Where do they disagree? Why?
> Is there a place for evolution in this account?

On a white board make three columns. One Column for Genesis 1, another for Genesis 2, and a third for evolution. Go through the order of how these different creation accounts say things happened. See where they line up and where they don't.

Example:
Genesis 1
- Earth
- Light
- Water
- Sky
- Land
- Plants
- Animals
- Humans

Genesis 2
- Earth
- Water
- Land/Garden
- Man
- Animals
- Woman

Evolution (Feel free to come up with your own order here)
    Earth
    Water
    Plants
    Creatures
    Humans

Ask them:

    How do you think creation actually happened?
    Does it affect what you think about God?

Close in Prayer

Homework
Answer:
What sort of responsibility do we have for caring for the earth?
Why do we have that responsibility?
What can we do to care for the earth?

Faith Diving Day 4
Naturalist or Forest Ranger
Location: Somewhere in Nature

Meet at the church

Opening Prayer
Begin with a word of prayer on the glory of God's creation.

Highs/Lows
Have the youth share a high event (good) and a low event (bad) from the last week.

Going Over The Homework
Ask the youth to get out their homework assignments. Ask them:

> What sort of responsibility do we have for caring for the earth
> Why do we have that responsibility?
> What can we do to care for the earth?

Field Trip
Go someplace with a naturalist or someone that works in nature or go to a zoo or some hike... get someone in the congregation to lead this that has some skill/knowledge in this area. Ask the guide to connect their knowledge about nature to God as much as possible.

Debrief on the way back about why someone would focus their life on caring for creation and whether or not God calls us to do this. Connect to passages like Jeremiah 2:7 (NRSV): "I brought you into a plentiful land to eat its fruits and its good things. But when you entered you defiled my land, and made my heritage an abomination."

If you have extra time... find a place for them to pick up trash or come up another way for them to care for creation.

Close in Prayer

Homework
Answer:
What sort of proof do you see out in the world that there is something more going on than we can see?
What are some unexplainable/less-believable things in the world that you believe in (ghosts/ufos/good luck/etc)

Faith Diving Day 5
Oddities of the World
Location: Inside

Opening Prayer
Begin with a word of prayer asking God to help us better understand the seemingly unexplainable parts of our world.

Highs/Lows
Have the youth share a high event (good) and a low event (bad) from the last week.

Going Over The Homework
Ask the youth to get out their homework assignments. Ask them:

> What sort of proof do you see in the world that there is more going on than we can see?
> What are some unexplainable/less-believable things in the world that you believe in (ghosts/ufos/good luck/etc)?

Mind over matter
Explain to the youth that there are many people that believe they can influence things with their minds, whether that is moving objects, affecting another's thoughts, or affecting nature. Ask them:

> Do you think we can influence things with our minds? Why/Why Not?
> If you could influence things with your mind would that prove that there is a spiritual world at work all around us or would it just be another one of those unexplainable physical thing?

Dice Control
Get some dice and allow the youth to try and Roll the dice with a specific number... tell them to try to influence the

dice. After awhile get the group back together and see if they can as a group influence one dice.

Sending a Word
Have one person go into another room and have them try to send their thoughts to everyone else. Have them make it one word.

My Dad and the Dogs
Story to share: Before cell phones, my dad was off with my mom in the middle of nowhere on vacation. They had left their two dogs behind and someone was supposedly watching those dogs. Suddenly, even though nothing had changed that my mom could see, my dad starts complaining that something is wrong back home and he needs to go find out what it is. He can't get past this feeling, so they drive the long way back to find that the dogs had gotten out right when my dad started feeling that things things were wrong. From more than one hundred miles away my dad knew that his dogs had gone missing. Ask them:

>Do you think activities or stories like that proves anything?
>Could occurrences like that be explained naturally?

A Soul
Inform that youth that some people say that you have a physical part of your body and then a more religiously inclined part of your body... they give it the name of the soul. Some people think that when you die, it is your soul that lives on. Ask them:

>Do you think you have a soul?
>How is a soul different than your body?

How much does a Soul Weigh?
Share this story with the youth from Mary Roach's book, Stiff: "Had you been visiting the Consumptives' Home in

April 1901, you might have been witness to a curious undertaking. A plump, meek-looking man of thirty-four, wearing wire-frame glasses and not as much hair as he once did, was stooped over the platform of an ornate Fairbanks scale, customizing the device with wooden supports and what appeared to be an army-style cot. The scale was an oversized commercial model, for weighing silk—no doubt a holdover from Jones's mercantile days.

"For the preceding four years of his life, Duncan Macdougall had been hatching a plan to prove the existence of the human soul. If, as most religions held, people leave their bodies behind at death and persist in the form of a soul, then mustn't this soul occupy space? "It is unthinkable," wrote Macdougall, "that personality and consciousness can be attributes of that which does not occupy space." And if they occupy space, he reasoned, they must have weight. "The question arose in my mind: Why not weigh a man at the very moment of death?" If the beam moved, and the body lost even a fraction of an ounce, he theorized, that loss might represent the soul's departure.

"Macdougall enlisted the help of two fellow physicians, Drs. Sproull and Grant, who chose not—or possibly weren't invited—to put their names on the research paper. The plan was to install a cot on the scale platform and then install a dying consumptive on the cot. Death from consumption is a still, quiet affair, and so it fit Macdougall's conditions "to a nicety," as he put it. "A consumptive dying after a long illness wasting his energies, dies with scarcely a movement to disturb the beam, their bodies are also very light, and we can be forewarned for hours that a consumptive is dying."

"At 5:30 p.m. on April 10, 1901, Patient 1's death—"my opportunity," Macdougall called it—was declared imminent. A male of ordinary build and "standard American temperament," he was wheeled from the ward and lifted onto the scale like a depleted bolt of silk. Macdougall summoned his partners. For three hours and forty minutes, the physicians watched the man fade. In place of the more usual bedside attitudes of grief and pity, the men assumed an air of breathless, intent expectancy.

"One doctor watched the man's chest; another, the movements of his face. Macdougall himself kept his eyes on the scale's indicator. "Suddenly, coincident with death," wrote Macdougall, "the beam end dropped with an audible stroke hitting against the lower limiting bar and remaining there with no rebound. The loss was ascertained to be three-fourths of an ounce."

Ask them:

> Does this prove anything?
> Do you think your soul actually weighs something?
> Are you just your body? Or is there more to you?

Ghosts for Next Time
Show them a clip from any ghost hunting show. There are a lot of them. Any one will do.

Close in Prayer

Homework
Answer:
Do you believe in ghosts?
What are they?
How do they fit into Christianity?

Faith Diving Day 6
Ghosts
Location: Haunted place

Meet at the church

If going to an outdoor "Haunted" location, have this conversation at the church. If Going to an indoor "Haunted" location have this conversation at the haunted location if possible.

Opening Prayer
Begin with a word of prayer asking for God's protection from anything that might seem scary.

Highs/Lows
Have the youth share a high event (good) and a low event (bad) from the last week.

Going Over The Homework
Ask the youth to get out their homework assignments. Ask them:

> Do you believe in ghosts?
> What are they?
> How do they fit into Christianity?

Ghosts
To talk about ghosts we first have to state what we are talking about... for the sake of this discussion let us say that a ghost is someone who has died yet their spirit lingers on to the point where they can somehow communicate with the living. Ask them:

> Have you heard any ghost stories? Did you believe them?

Share any ghost stories you know or have experienced. Share also a few famous ghost stories.

The Brown Lady

In 1936, a photographer taking pictures of the 300-year-old Raynham Hall in Norfolk, U.K., captured an image of an apparition floating down the stairs. It's one of the most famous ghost photos ever taken, although some experts believe it was caused by double exposure.

The manor, covering an area of 7,000 acres (2,833 hectares), has a long history of being haunted, and the BBC notes that the ghost may be of Lady Dorothy Townshend, the wife of the second viscount of the estate. She died in 1726, supposedly of smallpox, after having an affair, which her husband Lord Townshend had learned about before her death. She is said to still wander the manor dressed in brown.[4]

CCTV Ghost

Hampton Court Palace in Surrey, England, has a photogenic ghost of its own. In 2003, a CCTV camera caught an image of a skeletal figure, clad in centuries-old clothes, closing a sturdy fire door that had flung open. The ghost, nicknamed "skeletor," attracted a great deal of media attention.

"It wasn't just security staff who thought they were seeing things. A visitor wrote in the palace's visitor book on the [day that skeletor appeared on camera] that she too thought she had seen a ghost in that area," officials wrote on the Hampton Court Palace website.

Skeletor is not the only ghostly inhabitant of Hampton Court Palace. Catherine Howard, one of Henry VIII's wives, was imprisoned there and was supposedly dragged to her room, screaming all the way. The area that she haunts is called the "screaming gallery."

---

[4] https://www.livescience.com/48515-10-haunted-house-ghost-stories.html

Ask Them:

> Are ghosts proof of anything?
> Can ghosts fit into Christianity?

Leave for nearby haunted location, a cemetery always works.

Haunted Location
Before entering haunted location Pray something like:

> Angel of God, my guardian dear, To whom His love commits me here; Ever this Night be at my side, To light and guard, to rule and guide. God of power and might, as we journey forward to face the unknown, we pray for your constant protection, that we might leave here as we have come. We pray this in the power of your son's holy name. Amen[5]

Once "in" the location, explain to the youth that they are there to think about how something like ghosts could connect to their faith. They are there to think more deeply about whether or not they believe in things like ghosts.

In the haunted location... encourage the group to mostly stay together, but find their own space occasionally if they have the courage. Choose a few spots worthy of staking out as a group.

Take moments of silence in different areas to allow to feel for something "other." Make sure you give them plenty of opportunity to experience something.

Before leaving haunted location pray something like:

---

[5] https://www.xavier.edu/jesuitresource/online-resources/documents/GuardianAngelPrayer.pdf

> In the name of Jesus Christ, I command all human spirits to be bound to the confines of this place. I command all inhuman spirits to go where Jesus Christ tells you to go, for it is He who commands you. None may follow us. None may linger. By the power of Jesus Christ, we leave as we came.[6]

Go back to the church and debrief. Ask them:

> What did you experience?
> Are you any more likely to believe in ghosts now?
> If ghosts are real, does that mean life after death is more likely?

Close in Prayer

Homework
Familiarize yourself with the Old Testament in your Bible. Answer:
What is in the Old Testament?
Why do we call it old?
Are the stories in the Old Testament important?
What do these stories tell us?

---

[6] Celia Morgan, *The Paranormal Research and Investigation Handbook (CIPP: 2011), 20*

Faith Diving Day 7
Old Testament
Location: Church

Opening Prayer
Begin with a word of prayer thanking God for walking with people every step of the way through human history.

Highs/Lows
Have the youth share a high event (good) and a low event (bad) from the last week.

Going Over The Homework
Ask the youth to get out their homework assignments. Ask them:

> What is in the Old Testament?
> Why do we call it old?
> Are the stories in the Old Testament important?
> What do these stories tell us?

Hand out a single copy of a "New Testament Only" Bible and ask the youth what is missing in the Bible.

Old Testament Book Sorting Race
Have all the Old Testament books written down on two stacks of post-it notes (make sure they are out of order). Also have two stacks of Bibles (complete with Old Testament)… enough Bibles for all the youth to have one. The youth divide into two teams and then they have a minute to strategize (make sure you explain to the youth that Bibles have a table of contents)… and then they will race to see who can get the Old Testament books in order the fastest. Winner gets candy. After they finish the game, ask them:

> Why do you think there are so many books?
> What is the story that the Old Testament is trying to tell?

Finding Bible Passage Race

Make sure everyone has a Bible and give them a moment to flip through it. Then explain to them that we will be having a discussion, but in between each discussion we will see who can find a particular Bible passage the fastest and that person will get CANDY.

FIND GENESIS CHAPTER 3
Ask them:

> Who knows what this story is about?
> Do you know why it starts out our Bible?
> Do you agree with the reason for suffering as laid out in Genesis 3? Bad Fruit?

FIND EXODUS CHAPTER 20
Ask them:

> Who knows what this story is about?
> Why do you think it shows up so early in our Bible?
> Why do you think we hold onto some of the rules in the Old Testament, but not all?

FIND NUMBERS CHAPTER 11
Ask them:

> Who knows what this story is about?
> Why do you think it is in our Bible?
> Do you think you would complain if God gave you food on a daily basis?

FIND THE CRAZIEST STORY YOU CAN FIND IN ONE MINUTE (If they have their phones, they can use the internet)
Ask them:
> What did you find and what makes it crazy?
> Why is it important to read the Bible?
> Will read the Bible on your own?

Close in Prayer

Homework
Find a Bible in your house and bring it to the next meeting
Talk to your parents about the Bible and find out their thoughts on the Bible
Find the strangest Old Testament passage you can... winner gets candy (Can't reuse one from today).

Faith Diving Day 8
Old Testament (Bible) Interactive
Location: Church

Before the Meeting
Arrange for some older congregational members to meet with the youth and talk to them about what their Bibles mean to them.

Opening Prayer
Begin with a word of prayer thanking God for the elders in our church and all that they can teach us.

Highs/Lows
Have the youth share a high event (good) and a low event (bad) from the last week.

Going Over The Homework
Ask the youth to get out their homework assignments. Ask them:

> What were your parent's thoughts on the Bible
> What was the strangest Old Testament passage you could find?

Special Guests
Most churches have Bible studies largely made up of older members... if you do not have one of these, track down some "elders" of the church who find the Bible to be very important to them. Invite them to the second half of your faith diving time. Ask them to bring their personal Bible... the more well loved the better.

Invite the "elders" into the meeting at this point and explain to your group that these are people that see their Bible as important and many of them even choose to study the Bible on a weekly basis.

After everyone is seated ask the youth to think about why someone would choose to spend time being part of a group that studies the Bible EVERY WEEK. After the youth have given their answers... ask the Bible study group the same question.

Break Out Time
Depending on how many kids you have and how many Bible study people you have, try to break them out into as small a group as possible... one to one would be best, but take what you can get.

Give a hand out (see questions below) to the youth and have them bring their hand out and Bibles to a quiet place (preferably not in a room alone... but in something like a "fellowship hall" corner) and discuss the handout. The youth will be the interviewers. Give them around 10 minutes.

Hand Out Questions
How long have you had your Bible and why is it important to you?
Do you think all of the Bible is true? What do you do with passages you disagree with?
There are some strange passages in the Bible... what do you do with the weird passages?
Do you have any favorite Bible Passages?
Why do you go to church?
Do you have any questions for me?

Debrief
Thank the adults for their time and send them on their way. Get the kids back together to debrief what they heard... get them to answer the hand out questions as they heard the answers.

Soap Bible Study
Take that weirdest Bible passage from earlier and practice doing a Bible Study with it. Consider using a simple method like the "S.O.A.P" method or something similar.

WHAT DOES S.O.A.P. MEAN?
S-Scripture-Write out by hand the passage you are going to study.
O-Observation- What stands out in this passage, what do you notice, who do you notice, who is meant to be hearing these words?
A-Application- How can you apply this passage to your life, what is going saying to you through this Bible passage?
P-Prayer. If something has been shown to you or occurred to you while studying this passage, pray it back to God.

Hide Bibles
IF THERE IS EXTRA TIME... or the kids look bored... hide Bibles around the church... and have them find them... they get a piece of candy for every Bible they find.

Close in Prayer

Homework
Familiarize yourself with the book of Genesis and Exodus. At first just focus on the headings of each section.
If you have time, read as much of both books as you can.

Faith Diving Day 9
Bible Stories: Genesis-Exodus
Location: Inside

Opening Prayer
Begin with a word of prayer asking for God's help in unravelling confusing stories.

Highs/Lows
Have the youth share a high event (good) and a low event (bad) from the last week.

Going Over The Homework
Ask the youth to get out their homework assignments. Ask them:

> What did you notice while looking at Genesis and Exodus?
> Did you recognize any of the stories?
> What stories stuck out to you or seemed important?

The Bible Miniseries
Explain to the youth that the Bible is a collection of stories that help us to tell our own story about God in our lives. We have a lot of these stories because they helped people to better understand God.

With that in mind we are going to watch: The Bible: the history channel miniseries, episode 2.

Here is the link to it on amazon: http://www.amazon.com/gp/product/B00BW3PIMO/ref=dv_dp_ep2

The recap will tell the story of Genesis, and the episode will tell the story of Exodus. As we go through the miniseries we will pause the video to give them an opportunity to earn candy by finding the Bible passage the particular scene is based on.

Also, AND THIS IS IMPORTANT, let them know that it is more than okay to make fun of this show, to think critically about it and the stories... but try to get the gist of these stories because they have been very important to people.

Bible episode 1 recap can be found here:
http://www.history.com/shows/the-bible/videos/the-bible--recap-hour-1?m=5189719baf036&s=All&f=2&free=false

Scenes for Candy:

From Episode 1 Recap:
    In the Beginning (Genesis 1)
        Question: was it like this?
    Adam and Eve Disobeyed God (Genesis 3)
    Cain killed Abel (Genesis 4)
        Question: Do you think humans have always fought and will they always fight?
    Noah builds a boat (Genesis 7)
        Question: Did God flood the world?
    The call of Abraham (Genesis 12)
    Hagar (Genesis 16)
    Destruction of Sodom (Genesis 19)
        Question: Would God destroy a city?
    Three strangers visit Abraham (Genesis 18)
        Question: Who do you think these strangers were?
    Sacrifice of Isaac (Genesis 22)
        Question: How do you distinguish between mental health concerns and the call of God?

Stop the video as it begins the story in Exodus
    Father of many nations (Genesis 17:4)
        Question: Do you know we are known as an Abrahamic religion? (Judaism, Christianity, Islam... come from Abraham)

From Episode 2:
- Israel Enslaved (Exodus 1)
    - Question: Why would God allow this?
- Moses adopted (Exodus 2)
- Pharoah kills infants (Exodus 1)
    - Question: Did stories like this really happen?
- "He has deserted them."
    - Questions: What are we to do with events like this happening to followers of God?
- Moses kills (Exodus 2)
    - Question: What does it mean that one of the leaders of our faith was a murderer?
- Moses and the Burning bush (Exodus 3)
    - Question: Do things like this really happen?
- Let my people go (Exodus 5)
- The First Plague... water to blood (Exodus 7)
    - Question: Did this happen?
- Find the rest of the plagues (Frogs, gnats, flies, Exodus 8: livestock, boils, thunder and hail) Exodus 9; locust, darkness: Exodus 10)
- Passover (Exodus 12)
    - Question: Have you heard this story/holiday?
- Death of first borns (Exodus 12)
    - Question: What do you think of a God that would do that?
- Crossing the Red Sea (Exodus 14)
    - Question: Where are big miracles like this today?

Stop the video at the reception of the ten commandments, when they show the ark of the covenant.

Debrief
Ask them:

Is knowing these stories important?
Did these stories actually happened?
What did you think of that video?

Close in Prayer

Homework
Find the ten commandments in the Bible.
If you can find two versions you get a bonus prize.
If you can find three versions then you get an even bigger bonus.

Faith Diving Day 10
The Ten Commandments Scavenger Hunt
Location: In Cars

Meet at the church

Opening Prayer

Highs/Lows
Have the youth share a high event (good) and a low event (bad) from the last week.

Going Over The Homework
Ask the youth to get out their homework assignments. Did they find the ten commandments in the Bible? Did they find two versions to get a bonus prize? Did they find three versions to get an even bigger bonus?

Regular 10 Commandments
Exodus 20:2-17 and Deuteronomy 5:6-21 (NRSV)

I am the Lord your God, who brought you out of the land of Egypt, out of the house of slavery; you shall have no other gods before me.You shall not make for yourself an idol, whether in the form of anything that is in heaven above, or that is on the earth beneath, or that is in the water under the earth. You shall not bow down to them or worship them; for I the Lord your God am a jealous God, punishing children for the iniquity of parents, to the third and the fourth generation of those who reject me, but showing steadfast love to the thousandth generation of those who love me and keep my commandments.
You shall not make wrongful use of the name of the Lord your God, for the Lord will not acquit anyone who misuses his name.

Remember the sabbath day, and keep it holy. For six days you shall labour and do all your work. But the seventh day is a sabbath to the Lord your God; you shall not do any work—you, your son or your daughter, your male or female slave, your livestock, or the alien resident in your towns. For in six days the Lord made heaven and earth, the sea, and all that is in them, but rested the seventh day; therefore the Lord blessed the sabbath day and consecrated it.

Honor your father and your mother, so that your days may be long in the land that the Lord your God is giving you.

You shall not murder.

You shall not commit adultery.

You shall not steal.

You shall not bear false witness against your neighbor.

You shall not covet your neighbor's house

You shall not covet your neighbor's wife, or male or female slave, or ox, or donkey, or anything that belongs to your neighbor.

Third Version
Tablet Smash, Tablet Remade (Exodus 34) (NRSV)

Then Moses turned and went down from the mountain, carrying the two tablets of the covenant in his hands, tablets that were written on both sides, written on the front and on the back. The tablets were the work of God, and the writing was the writing of God, engraved upon the tablets. As soon as he came near the camp and saw the calf and the dancing, Moses' anger burned hot, and he threw the tablets from his hands and broke them at the foot of the mountain. He took the calf that they had made, burned it with fire, ground it to powder, scattered it on the water, and made the Israelites drink it.

The Lord said to Moses, 'Cut two tablets of stone like the former ones, and I will write on the tablets the words that were on the former tablets, which you broke. Be ready in the morning, and come up in the morning to Mount Sinai and present yourself there to me, on the top of the mountain. No one shall come up with you, and do not let anyone be seen throughout all the mountain; and do not let flocks or herds graze in front of that mountain.' So Moses cut two tablets of stone like the former ones; and he rose early in the morning and went up on Mount Sinai, as the Lord had commanded him, and took in his hand the two tablets of stone.

Exodus 34:12-26
1. Take care not to make a covenant with the inhabitants of the land to which you are going, or it will become a snare among you. You shall tear down their altars, break their pillars, and cut down their sacred poles (for you shall worship no other god, because the Lord, whose name is Jealous, is a jealous God). You shall not make a covenant with the inhabitants of the land, for when they prostitute themselves to their gods and sacrifice to their gods, someone among them will invite you, and you will eat of the sacrifice. And you will take wives from among their daughters for your sons, and their daughters who prostitute themselves to their gods will make your sons also prostitute themselves to their gods.
2. You shall not make cast idols.
3. You shall keep the festival of unleavened bread. For seven days you shall eat unleavened bread, as I commanded you, at the time appointed in the month of Abib; for in the month of Abib you came out from Egypt.
4. All that first opens the womb is mine, all your male livestock, the firstborn of cow and sheep. The firstborn of a donkey you shall redeem with a lamb, or if you will not redeem it you shall break its neck. All the firstborn of your

sons you shall redeem.

5. No one shall appear before me empty-handed.
6. For six days you shall work, but on the seventh day you shall rest; even in ploughing time and in harvest time you shall rest.
7. You shall observe the festival of weeks, the first fruits of wheat harvest, and the festival of ingathering at the turn of the year. Three times in the year all your males shall appear before the Lord God, the God of Israel. For I will cast out nations before you, and enlarge your borders; no one shall covet your land when you go up to appear before the Lord your God three times in the year.
8. You shall not offer the blood of my sacrifice with leaven, and the sacrifice of the festival of the passover shall not be left until the morning.
9. The best of the first fruits of your ground you shall bring to the house of the Lord your God.
10. You shall not boil a kid in its mother's milk.

Discussion
Ask them:

> What is the real 10 commandments?
> What do you see as the value of the ten commandments

Photo Scavenger Hunt
Break into teams to take part in a Ten Commandments Scavenger Hunt. Have the youth driven around town to take pictures of ten commandment related things. They will also need to answer questions for each item. The first team back will win the prize. Print out the scavenger hunt clues for each car. Each car needs at least one smart phone for picture taking.

1a. Ten Commandments on the Wall

Take a picture of a the ten commandments posted on a wall. (OK to skip if one is not easily accessible)

Question:
Why do you think people find these commandments important enough to put on a wall?

1b. "I am the Lord your God, who brought you out of the land of Egypt, out of the house of bondage. You shall have no other gods before Me."

Take a picture of a bank.

Questions:
What are the things we sometimes value over God? (Examples: Money, Video Games, Clothes, Friends, ect.)

Why is it important to put God first?

2. "You shall not take the name of the Lord your God in vain, for the Lord will not hold him guiltless who takes His name in vain."

Take a picture of something that would make someone take the Lord's name in vain.

Questions:
What does it mean to take the Lord's name in vain?

Why is it a bad thing to take the Lord's name in vain?

3. "Remember the Sabbath day, to keep it holy. Six days you shall labor and do all your work, but the seventh day is the Sabbath of the Lord your God. In it you shall do no work: you, nor your son, nor your daughter, nor your male servant, nor your female servant, nor your cattle, nor your

stranger who is within your gates. For in six days the Lord made the heavens and the earth, the sea, and all that is in them, and rested the seventh day. Therefore the Lord blessed the Sabbath day and hallowed it."

Take a picture of a place that is really relaxing... a beautiful spot in nature.

Questions:
Why do you think the sabbath is important?

Why is it important to take time to rest?

4. "Honor your father and your mother, that your days may be long upon the land which the Lord your God is giving you."

Take a picture of an older person that you don't know... they should be no less than sixty, but do not ask their age... tell them you need to take a picture about honoring those that have gone before us.

Questions:
Why should we honor our father and mother?

Why should we honor and give respect to people that are older than us?

5. "You shall not murder."

Take a picture of artillery or a military related item

Questions:
How does this commandment relate to war?

Is killing always wrong?

6. "You shall not commit adultery."

Take a picture of a couple that has been married for a long time.

Questions:
What do you think is the key to a long, healthy relationship?

What does it mean to love someone?

What does it mean to you that we are supposed to love everyone?

7. "You shall not steal."

Take a picture of something at the store you can't afford, but really want.

Questions:
Is there ever a time where stealing is okay?

Why is stealing wrong?

8. "You shall not bear false witness against your neighbor."

Take a picture of a courthouse (if your courthouse has a "lady justice statue" have them take a picture of that instead).

Questions:
Why is keeping your word important?

Have you ever been lied to? How did it feel?

9. "You shall not covet your neighbor's house."

Go to the house of every person in the car and take a picture of the neighbor's house.

Questions:
What does your neighbor have to do with you?

Does it matter what thoughts are in your head if you don't act on them?

10. "You shall not covet your neighbor's wife, nor his male servant, nor his female servant, nor his ox, nor his donkey, nor anything that is your neighbor's."

Take a picture of a donkey (or horse if you can't find a donkey... and if you can't find a donkey... have the kids bring up something that someone has that they always covet and take a picture of that).

Questions:
Why is wanting what someone else has a bad thing?

Have you ever wanted something that someone else had? How did that make you feel about them?

Now quickly (AND SAFELY) get back to the church, for the first team that gets back gets the prize.

Debrief
If you have time... when everyone gets back ask them:

>Are the ten commandments important?
>What is the most important commandment?
>What happens if you break a commandment?

What does it mean to receive forgiveness?

Close in Prayer

Homework
Locate a children's Bible and flip through the stories that are from the Old Testament.
Answer:
Why do you think they chose the stories from the Old Testament that they did?
What are those stories trying to tell us?
Did they leave out any stories they shouldn't have?

Faith Diving Day 11
Other Old Testament Books
Location: Inside

Opening Prayer

Highs/Lows
Have the youth share a high event (good) and a low event (bad) from the last week.

Going Over The Homework
Ask the youth to get out their homework assignments. Ask them:

> Why do you think the children's Bible compilers chose the stories from the Old Testament that they did?
> What are those stories trying to tell us?
> Did they leave out any stories they shouldn't have?

Judaism
Ask the youth who the Old Testament stories are about. Yes they are about the people of God... our people... but more specifically it is about Israel, the Jewish people. Ask them what they know about the historical Jewish people and Judaism in general.

The Bible Miniseries
Tell them you are going to show them an episode from the miniseries, "The Bible." The Episode is called Survival. It is about the two biggest points of Jewish history following the "origin stories." These are the stories of king David and the Babylonian captivity. Stories that shape much of who the Jewish people are now and what they hoped for. Here is a link: https://www.amazon.com/Bible-The-tv-Series/dp/B00I83WKFE/ref=pd_sbs_74_img_2?_encoding=UTF8&psc=1&refRID=6N6DZ0YQEM332SQ17HP9

As usual they get candy if they can find the stories in their Bibles. Play the "Previously...." Clip as well. Pause the show when you want them to guess the Bible passage. They are going to need more time to find the appropriate passages than in the previous viewing.

:45 Joshua brings them into the promised land (Jericho is ours!) Joshua 6:20

1:02 Brutal Opposition from the Philistines 1 Samuel 7:7

Question: Why do God's people not have it easier?

1:21 Samson Brings the walls down Judges 16:29

1:43 Saul made first king 1 Samuel 10

3:02 Saul sacrifices instead of Samuel 1 Samuel 13:9

Question: Why would God care if a priest did something rather than a regular person? Also... what do you think of "God's Command" to kill everyone?"

5:15 God Forsakes Saul 1 Samuel 15

Question: Does God forsake people, reject them? Why would go do that?

7:47 David is anointed 1 Samuel 16

Question: Who is David? Why is David important for us today? Notice where David was from? (Bethlehem)

10:55 Thy rod and staff they comfort me. Psalm 23

Question: Why are they doing this right now? (We say that David wrote many of the Psalms. They are meant to comfort in times of difficult, help us to celebrate, help us to live out all emotions)

12:25 David Strikes down Goliath 1 Samuel 17

Question: What is the point of this story?

16:35 100 dead philistines 1 Samuel 18:25

After David Flees skip to...48:53 as a new episode starts. See if they can find any stories based off the quick images....

Joshua brings them into the promised land (Jericho is ours!) Joshua 6:20
Sacrifice of Isaac Genesis 22
Moses parts the red sea Exodus 14
David Delivers Jerusalem 2nd Samuel 5
52:50 Surrender to Nebekenezzer or die Jeremiah 38:18 Place yourself under the yoke of Babylon Jeremiah 27:11
Question: Why is he wearing that yoke? (Prophetic Play Acting)
1:00 Stop.

Babylonian Captivity Discussion

This begins an era known as the Babylonian captivity... things to talk about:
God's Temple destroyed. God's house.
Shift in thinking that the good were rewarded and the bad punished because everyone is punished. Book of Job is about the exile.
Why would God allow that to happen to God's chosen people? Why does God allow bad things to happen?

Dramatic Reenactment

If you have time... divide into groups and have them act out any of the stories they saw today. They need to make it dramatic... with props, but after they have acted it out they need to explain why the story is important to us today... what it tells us today.

Close in Prayer

Homework

Go online and research Judaism.
Find out something you didn't know about judaism.
Find out one interesting/strange/odd fact about modern day Judaism... most interesting wins.

Faith Diving Day 12
Judaism/Synagogue
Location: Inside and then at Synagogue

Opening Prayer

Highs/Lows
Have the youth share a high event (good) and a low event (bad) from the last week.

Going Over The Homework
Ask the youth to get out their homework assignments. Ask them:

> What did you find out about Judaism?
> What interesting fact did you learn about modern day Judaism?
> How is Christianity related to Judaism?

Israel
Have everyone go get a Bible and give a prize to the first person that can find the word "Israel" in the Bible. Ask them:

> What is Israel?
> What have you heard about Israel in the world today?
> Is Israel in the Bible the same as Israel on a map today?
> Does Christianity replace Judaism?

History of Judaism[7]
"Judaism is the world's oldest monotheistic religion, dating back nearly 4,000 years. Followers of Judaism believe in one God who revealed himself through ancient prophets. The history of Judaism is essential to understanding the Jewish faith, which has a rich heritage of law, culture and tradition.

---

[7] https://www.history.com/topics/religion/judaism

"Jewish people believe there's only one God who has established a covenant—or special agreement—with them. Their God communicates to believers through prophets and rewards good deeds while also punishing evil. Most Jews (with the exception of a few groups) believe that their Messiah hasn't yet come—but will one day.

"Jewish people worship in holy places known as synagogues, and their spiritual leaders are called rabbis. The six-pointed Star of David is the symbol of Judaism. Today, there are about 14 million Jews worldwide. Most of them live in the United States and Israel. Traditionally, a person is considered Jewish if his or her mother is Jewish."

Jewish Texts
"The Jewish sacred text is called the Tanakh or the "Hebrew Bible." It includes the same books as the Old Testament in the Christian Bible, but they're placed in a slightly different order. The Torah—the first five books of the Tanakh—outlines laws for Jews to follow. It's sometimes also referred to as the Pentateuch."

Ask Them:

> What do you think of Judaism as a separate religion from Christianity?
> Do you think it is important to know about Judaism?

Synagogue Visit
Arrange with a Synagogue leader to come and visit. If possible try to schedule some time for the students to talk with the Rabbi after the service.

Before you Leave
Remind kids about being courteous and respectful
Remind kids that they may have to put on different

clothing at the synagogue (check with synagogue leaders about this).
Let parents know when you will return.

Debrief Back at the Church
When you get back to the church, if there's time, ask them:

> What was different at the synagogue vs. our church?
> Why do you think they worship the way that they do?
> Is there anything we can learn from how they worship?
> Do you think they are worshipping our God or another God or no God?

Close in Prayer

Homework
Think about topics that are hard to talk about, things we call "hot button" issues, things that can trigger immediate and intense reactions from people when discussed. What issues in our society are the hardest for you to talk about or understand? Write down some initial thoughts on those issues.

Faith Diving Day 13
Hot Button
Location: Inside

Opening Prayer

Highs/Lows
Have the youth share a high event (good) and a low event (bad) from the last week.

Going Over The Homework
Ask the youth to get out their homework assignments. Ask them:
> What issues did you write down that are the hardest for you to talk about or understand?

Hot Button Issues Game
Play a modified version of hot potato. Get the kids into a circle and have them pass around a modified soccer ball. Tape various hot button topics onto the different pentagons/hexagons. Each time they catch the ball they have to call out the hot button topic they see first and then they have to pass on the ball without dropping it. Whenever time runs out or someone drops the ball, the person that did not get a chance to pass on the ball has to be the first to say their thoughts about the hot button issue that was last called out. After the first person answers, everyone in the group shares their views by going around the circle.

Before you begin, make sure they understand what each hot button topic means. Let them know that answers to these topics are not to be shared outside the group so people feel they have the freedom to share. Let them know that many of the topics they will get into today have deep meaning for many people within the group and they need to work to be respectful. Feel free to add the issues you would like your group to talk about, but here are some potential discussion topics:

Suicide
LGBTQIA
Premarital Sex
Abortion
Racism
Diversity
Gender Equality
Bullying
Drugs and Alcohol
Gun Control
War
Immigration
Euthanasia
Death Penalty
Environmentalism

Debrief
Have the youth talk about their experience of the game and what it was like to talk about those hard things. See if there were any issues they wished the group had talked about. Take the time to talk about those.

Close in Prayer

Homework
Think about your big questions about God, reasons you struggle to believe in God, or any confusions you might have. Try to stump the Faith Diving leader with your odd and ridiculous questions!

Faith Diving Day 14
Big Questions
Location: Inside

Opening Prayer

Highs/Lows
Have the youth share a high event (good) and a low event (bad) from the last week.

Going Over The Homework
Ask the youth to get out their homework assignments. Ask them:
> What are your big questions about God, reasons you struggle to believe in God, or any confusions you have?
> Did you come up with any odd or ridiculous questions to stump your Faith Diving leader?

Big Questions
Hopefully they will come up with enough questions organically so that you don't have to make use of the below list, but try to prompt them to ask their own questions.

> What makes Christianity, Christianity? What is difficult about being a Christian?
> Is Baptism necessary? What about those who don't get Baptized?
> Is Communion really the body and blood of Jesus? Are you okay eating and drinking that?
> What's the hardest part of the Jesus story for you to believe?
> What about other religions/denominations? How do we know who is right?
> Heaven/Hell? Are they real? Who goes to Heaven? Who goes to Hell?
> Do you really have a Holy Spirit within you? Shouldn't you make the right decision more often?

How do we know we can trust what is in the Bible?
Can the Bible tell the future?
Is going to church really important?
Should we even have churches?
Shouldn't we just sleep in on Sundays and talk to God later?
What should churches be doing with their time?
Will you go to church when you or older?
Why do bad things happen to good people?
If God is so perfect, then why did God create something so imperfect allowing pain, suffering and daily atrocities?
How can someone be God's son and God at the same time?
Couldn't God have "saved" us another way than the cross?
Why doesn't God heal more people?
Why do some prayers seem to go unanswered?
Why doesn't God speak to us more clearly?
Why doesn't God just show himself to everyone at once so that everyone can believe?
If God created everything, why did God allow for AIDS, covid, cancer, and every other terrible thing?

Faith Letters

If confirmation day is approaching, talk to "graduating" youth about their faith letters. All the graduating Faith Divers are to write a letter to present on the Sunday of their graduation. Invite them to be open and honest about where their faith is at and where they think it is going.

Have them email these letters to you (the leader) to read and, no matter what, prompt them to say a little more and push them to be even more honest. They know what we want them to say, but we want to actually hear where they are.

Faith Diving, Confirmation Ritual
Explain to the graduating youth what sort of ritual your church uses for confirmation so they are prepared. Also, make sure to remind them that they are welcome to continue with faith diving.

For kids not graduating... two weeks after the graduation we will go see as "religious" a movie as we can find in theaters.

Close in Prayer

Homework
For the graduates, their homework is their faith letter. For the non-graduates encourage them to think about how we can learn about God, not just from religious things, but also from nearly anything... including a big box office movie that on the surface has almost nothing to do with God.

Faith Diving Day 15
Faith Diver Graduation
Location: Church

Faith Letter
All the Faith Divers are to write a letter to read in front of the church on the Sunday of their graduation. Invite them to be open and honest about where their faith is at and where they think it is going. At my church we have this faith diving sharing moment as the sermon for the day.

For youth who have a strong fear of speaking in public we have them record a video to share with the congregation.

Ritual
After the Faith Diver Faith Letter sharing time, hold whatever "Affirmation of Faith" ritual your church is accustomed to using.

Faith Diving Day 16
Movie for non-graduates
Location: Movie Theatre

Meet at the church

Opening Prayer

Highs/Lows
Have the youth share a high event (good) and a low event (bad) from the last week.

Before Movie Conversation
Ask the youth:
> What are they hoping to learn more about next year?
> What helped them this year to learn more about their faith?
> What confused them this year?

Go See a Movie
It can be a faith based movie if one is available, but can be anything. Make sure you debrief after the movie is over.

Close in Prayer

End Year 1

Year 2
Christianity and New Testament

Faith Diving Day 17
Christianity Overview
Location: Inside

Opening Prayer

Highs/Lows
Have the youth share a high event (good) and a low event (bad) from the last week.

Welcome in the New Class.
Welcome the returning students. Explain the nature of faith diving.

Ice Breaker 1000 Bill Exchange
For this game you need to make your own money on your computer (be sure it's clearly phony or it might be a federal offense). Give each person 10 of the bills. They are to try to win as many as possible from their peers by challenging them one on one doing any kind of competition that they can do safely/ethically.

Suggestions:
Thumb wrestling
Rock, paper, scissors
Flipping a coin
Staring Contest (No Blinking)

Rules:
You must know the name of the person you are challenging.
With each challenge you must learn one new thing about the person.
You must accept any challenge
Sudden death, no two out of three

Debrief
After they have gotten to know each and had a good amount of time to win/lose, ask them:

> Is luck real and what causes luck if it is real?
> Can Christians be competitive?
> Can Christians gamble?
> What can Christians do?
> What can't Christians do?
> How do you know what Christians can/can't do? Is it always easy to tell?
> What does it mean to love your neighbor as yourself?
> Were you loving to your neighbor while you were competing?
> Why do we care about loving our neighbor as ourself?

Go into the sanctuary.

Discussion about Christianity
Give them a chance to look around the sanctuary and then ask them:

> What makes Christianity, Christianity?
> What are the parts of the sanctuary that are required for it to be a Christian worship space.

Allow them to name the various parts of the worship space that are important to them and their faith, make sure you "help them" to get the big ones. Suggestions:

The Baptismal Font
Have water present in a pitcher, pour the water into the font, run your hands through the water. Invite them to stand around it and run their hands through it. Ask them:

> What is this for?
> What do we do with it?
> What does a baptism ritual look like?

Take them through the Baptismal rite as it occurs at your congregation. Ask them:

> But why do we do baptism?
> What is gained from it?
> Is it necessary for salvation?

Remind them that being baptized is like putting on a cloak of Christ (if you have a robe nearby, use it to give a very visual demonstration). Remind them that all the bad things they are doing are forgotten because when God looks at you, God sees Jesus (the robe), instead of the bad.

Remembrance of baptism reminds us how much we are protected and cared for. It does not suddenly make you a sinless person who never doubts, or fears, or makes mistakes. It is simply a marker, a claiming, you are completely and truly a child of God now and that adoption is for life. Baptism is not about exclusion, saying that those who don't have it are outside of God's love, it is instead about saying that these specific people that have received this baptist have explicitly and clearly been marked for God.

The Altar
Have communion elements present. Walk them through how communion is done at your congregation. Allow them to eat the bread and drink the wine directly from the altar. Explain to them why communion is important to you. Ask them:

> Why is communion important to you?
> Is it important?
> What do you think is gained out of it?

Talk about the candles and the significance of lighting those candles.

Talk about offering plates, what it means to tithe and offer a portion of what we have up to God.

Lectern
Have a Bible present on the Lectern. Explain why the Bible is important to you. Ask them:

> What do you think about the Bible?
> Is the Bible important?
> Why should people read it?

Cross
Give them a second to look up at the cross in front of the church. Ask them:

> What does the cross mean to you?

Pews
Ask them what is special about the pews? They probably won't offer up much, but tell them about the "priesthood of all believers" (that we are all able to connect directly with God, not just the pastor, and we are all given a calling to spread God's message through our unique gifts).

Blessing
Have them bless one another… have them mark the sign of the cross on their neighbors forehead or hand and then say something nice that they hope will happen to them. After they bless each other, talk about how they did a very "priestly" action.

After they have labeled most of the important parts of the ritual space, ask them:

> Why is Christianity important to you or is it?
> Who was Jesus? What did Jesus accomplish? Who is Jesus for you?
> What do people say about Christians? About the church? Are they right?

Close in Prayer

Homework
For next time, have them write down answers to the following questions:
Who is God to you?
Who is Jesus to you?
Who is the Holy Spirit to you?
What is a church, in your opinion?
Why go to a worship service?
What is Lutheranism?
What is baptism and why is it important?
What is communion and why is it important?
What is the Bible and why is it important?
What is the New Testament and why is it important?
Find one story you like from the New Testament and explain why you like it.

Have them BRING A BIBLE WITH THEM NEXT TIME.

Faith Diving Day 18
New Testament Overview/Jesus Story
Location: Inside

Meet in a room where you can watch a movie.

Opening Prayer

Highs/Lows
Have the youth share a high event (good) and a low event (bad) from the last week.

Going Over The Homework
Ask the youth to get out their homework assignments. Ask them:
> Who is God to you?
> Who is Jesus to you?
> Who is the Holy Spirit to you?
> What is a church, in your opinion?
> Why go to a worship service?
> What is Lutheranism?
> What is baptism and why is it important?
> What is communion and why is it important?
> What is the Bible and why is it important?
> What is the New Testament and why is it important?
> What one story from the New Testament did you find?
> What is a Gospel? Why are there so many of them? Why don't they agree?
> What kind of Bible did you bring? Do you read it? Where did it come from?

The Bible Miniseries
Watch "The Bible" Together.
Get a copy of the last episode of "Bible Miniseries" which is called either courage or the passion part 2... you can find it on Amazon at: http://www.amazon.com/gp/product/B00C4VDA2S/ref=dv_dp_ep10

Explain to the youth that we are going to try to find passages from the New Testament while watching the review of previous episodes and the current episode. Give out candy rewards when they are able to find them. Remind them that it is more than appropriate to make fun of the acting or story telling at any point.

Mary you will soon give birth to a son, the son of God.
    Where? Matthew 1:21, Luke 1:31
    Who says this?
    What is an angel? Are Angels Real?

Jesus Baptism
    Where? Matthew 3:13-17, John 1:29-34
    Why was Jesus baptized? Did he need Baptism?
    Who was John the Baptist? What does it mean to prepare the way?

Get up and walk
    Where? Mark 2:9, Matthew 9:5, John 5:8
    Why don't more healing miracles happen today?
    Do we have the power to do something like this?

Flipping over tables in the temple... you cannot serve God and money
    Where? Matthew 6:24, Luke 16:13
    Why does Jesus say that you cannot serve God and money?
    What is the danger of money?

Father forgive them, they know not what they do
    Where? Luke 23:34
    Why is forgiving someone so hard?
    Why does Jesus say, Father forgive them, instead of I forgive them?

Mary at the tomb
    Where? John 20:11

Do you think Jesus really came back?

Mary reports that the tomb is open
    Where? John 20
    Why wouldn't they believe her?

Peter goes to see the tomb for himself
    Where? John 20
    Ask them if they've heard of the Shroud of Turin

This is my body, this is my blood
    Where? Matthew 26:26, Luke 22:19
    Why did they celebrate communion?
    Why did Jesus appear after they took communion?

Thomas stop doubting and believe
    Where? John 20:24-29
    Crucifixion scars are wrong

Jesus ascends to heaven.
    Where? Mark 16:19, Luke 24:51, Acts 1:6-12
    Where did he go?

Close in Prayer

Homework
Look at any of the first four books of the New Testament (the Gospels... Matthew, Mark, Luke and John) and choose one book to look closely at. While paying special attention to what is said by Jesus in the Gospel you chose, try to answer the following questions:
Who was Jesus and what did he do that was important?
Who is Jesus to you?
What does it mean to be a follower of Jesus in the Gospel you picked?
What have you always wondered about... when it came to Jesus? Or have you never wondered anything about Jesus?

Faith Diving Day 19
Jesus and the Gospels
Location: Inside

Opening Prayer

Highs/Lows
Have the youth share a high event (good) and a low event (bad) from the last week.

Going Over The Homework
Ask the youth to get out their homework assignments. Ask them:
> Which Gospel did you choose?
> Who was Jesus and what did he do that was important?
> Who is Jesus to you?
> What does it mean to be a follower of Jesus in the Gospel you picked?
> What have you always wondered about... when it came to Jesus? Or have you never wondered anything about Jesus?

Jesus Pictures
Do an internet search for images of Jesus. There are plenty of good ones. Choose a variety of them, print them out in color and hide the pictures of Jesus all around the church.

Tell the youth they have to do two things. 1) See how many pictures of Jesus they can find hidden in the church (Count them). 2) Find ONLY ONE to keep, bring it back to the group, and explain why they chose the picture of Jesus that they did. Afterward, ask them:

> Why was Jesus shown the way that he was into those pictures?
> Why isn't Jesus the same for everyone?

Nativity Time
Show the youth this video where kids re-tell the story of Jesus' birth: htttps://youtu.be/suowe2czxcA

Ask the youth to tell you about the nativity, the birth of Jesus... from memory.

Now ask the youth what Gospel their particular retelling comes from. Then ask them to find for you the Jesus birth story from the Gospel of Mark. Then ask them to find for you the Jesus birth story from the Gospel of John. The problem: no Mark or John birth story.

Nativity Act Out
IF TIME, split into groups and have the youth act out either the Matthew or Luke Nativity story as it is written. Best acting performance gets candy.

Matthew Story (Matthew 1:18-2:12 NRSV)
18 Now the birth of Jesus the Messiah took place in this way. When his mother Mary had been engaged to Joseph, but before they lived together, she was found to be with child from the Holy Spirit. 19 Her husband Joseph, being a righteous man and unwilling to expose her to public disgrace, planned to dismiss her quietly. 20 But just when he had resolved to do this, an angel of the Lord appeared to him in a dream and said, "Joseph, son of David, do not be afraid to take Mary as your wife, for the child conceived in her is from the Holy Spirit. 21 She will bear a son, and you are to name him Jesus, for he will save his people from their sins." 22 All this took place to fulfill what had been spoken by the Lord through the prophet: 23 "Look, the virgin shall conceive and bear a son, and they shall name him Emmanuel," which means, "God is with us." 24 When Joseph awoke from sleep, he did as the angel of the Lord commanded him; he took her as his wife, 25 but had no marital relations with her until she had borne a son; and he named him Jesus.

In the time of King Herod, after Jesus was born in Bethlehem of Judea, wise men from the East came to Jerusalem, 2 asking, "Where is the child who has been born king of the Jews? For we observed his star at its rising, and have come to pay him homage." 3 When King Herod heard this, he was frightened, and all Jerusalem with him; 4 and calling together all the chief priests and scribes of the people, he inquired of them where the Messiah was to be born. 5 They told him, "In Bethlehem of Judea; for so it has been written by the prophet: 'And you, Bethlehem, in the land of Judah, are by no means least among the rulers of Judah; for from you shall come a ruler who is to shepherd my people Israel.'"

7 Then Herod secretly called for the wise men and learned from them the exact time when the star had appeared. 8 Then he sent them to Bethlehem, saying, "Go and search diligently for the child; and when you have found him, bring me word so that I may also go and pay him homage." 9 When they had heard the king, they set out; and there, ahead of them, went the star that they had seen at its rising, until it stopped over the place where the child was. 10 When they saw that the star had stopped, they were overwhelmed with joy. 11 On entering the house, they saw the child with Mary his mother; and they knelt down and paid him homage. Then, opening their treasure chests, they offered him gifts of gold, frankincense, and myrrh. 12 And having been warned in a dream not to return to Herod, they left for their own country by another road.

Luke Story (Luke 2:1-20 NRSV)
(THERE IS ALSO MORE TO THE STORY IN LUKE 1)
In those days a decree went out from Emperor Augustus that all the world should be registered. 2 This was the first registration and was taken while Quirinius was governor of Syria. 3 All went to their own towns to be registered. 4 Joseph also went from the town of Nazareth in Galilee to Judea, to the city of David called Bethlehem, because he was descended from the house and family of

David. 5 He went to be registered with Mary, to whom he was engaged and who was expecting a child. 6 While they were there, the time came for her to deliver her child. 7 And she gave birth to her firstborn son and wrapped him in bands of cloth, and laid him in a manger, because there was no place for them in the inn.

8 In that region there were shepherds living in the fields, keeping watch over their flock by night. 9 Then an angel of the Lord stood before them, and the glory of the Lord shone around them, and they were terrified. 10 But the angel said to them, "Do not be afraid; for see—I am bringing you good news of great joy for all the people: 11 to you is born this day in the city of David a Savior, who is the Messiah, the Lord. 12 This will be a sign for you: you will find a child wrapped in bands of cloth and lying in a manger." 13 And suddenly there was with the angel a multitude of the heavenly host, praising God and saying, 14 "Glory to God in the highest heaven, and on earth peace among those whom he favors!"

15 When the angels had left them and gone into heaven, the shepherds said to one another, "Let us go now to Bethlehem and see this thing that has taken place, which the Lord has made known to us." 16 So they went with haste and found Mary and Joseph, and the child lying in the manger. 17 When they saw this, they made known what had been told them about this child; 18 and all who heard it were amazed at what the shepherds told them. 19 But Mary treasured all these words and pondered them in her heart. 20 The shepherds returned, glorifying and praising God for all they had heard and seen, as it had been told them.

Debrief
Ask them:
> Why do you think the Gospel stories are different?
> Should we keep the nativity stories separated or combine them?
> What do these 4 nativity stories (2 with them, 2 without them) tell you about our Gospels?

Does the Bible become less trustworthy because the stories are not the same?
How much can we know for sure about Jesus? Does this bother you?

Close in Prayer

Homework
Flip through the book of Acts in your Bible and find out what characters are in it and what sort of stories run through it. Also, consider faith healings... why do you think some people get miraculous healings and others don't?

Ask the youth (if they want) to bring a stuffed animal to be "healed" next class time.

Faith Diving Day 20
Acts (Peter, Paul, Holy Spirit) Faith healings
Location: Inside

Opening Prayer

Highs/Lows
Have the youth share a high event (good) and a low event (bad) from the last week.

Going Over The Homework
Ask the youth to get out their homework assignments. Ask them:

> What stood out to you about the book of Acts?
> Why do you think some people get miraculous healings and others don't?

The Bible Miniseries
Watch "The Bible" Together.
Get a copy of the last episode of "Bible Miniseries" which is called either courage or the passion part 2... you can find it on Amazon at: http://www.amazon.com/gp/product/B00C4VDA2S/ref=dv_dp_ep10

Explain to the youth that we are going to try to find passages from the New Testament while watching the review of previous episodes and the current episode. Have teams break into groups and tell them that the winning group will get all the candy and get to decide if they share or not. Remind them that it is more than appropriate to make fun of the acting or story telling at any point.

Speaking in different languages....
>   Where? Acts 2:4
>   What does it mean to speak in tongues
>   What is the Holy Spirit?
>   What does the Holy Spirit do?

Apostles heal many
    Where? Acts 3:6

Faith Healing Discussion
Remind the youth that Paul was healed through prayer, Aeneas was healed through prayer. Ask them:

    Do you think those healings actually happened?
    Do you think people get healed today through prayer?
    Why do you think more people don't get healed?
    Do you have the power to do a faith healing?

Show a video of a televangelist faith healing. There are a lot of them, you can use the beginning of this one: http://www.youtube.com/watch?v=jzAHr0cKz7Q (Stop at about 40 Seconds). Ask them:

    Do you know what a televangelist is?
    Do you think they are really healing people?

Faith Healings Test (Stuffed Animal)
Inform the youth that they are going to do their best televangelist faith healing… on a stuffed animal. The one that does the best, most over the top, faith healing will get a prize.

Invite them up, two at a time… to have a "healing face off." Have both performances scored (adults hold up score cards) and winner moves onto the next round. Overall winner gets candy.

Faith Healing Test Discussion Continued
Ask the youth:

    Is that how we are really supposed to try to help people?
    Is that how Jesus would do a faith healing?

How would Jesus do a faith healing?
How should you?
What is it about us that might give us the power to do some big miraculous thing (Answer: Holy Spirit).
What is the Holy Spirit to you?
Do you think you have any special gifts from God? (Answer: YES!)
How are we supposed to use those gifts?

Who is Paul?
Tell the youth about Paul in our New Testament, who is believed to have written nearly half of the New Testament. Around 14 books.

Read Acts 9:1-22 (NRSV)
9 Meanwhile Saul, still breathing threats and murder against the disciples of the Lord, went to the high priest 2 and asked him for letters to the synagogues at Damascus, so that if he found any who belonged to the Way, men or women, he might bring them bound to Jerusalem. 3 Now as he was going along and approaching Damascus, suddenly a light from heaven flashed around him. 4 He fell to the ground and heard a voice saying to him, "Saul, Saul, why do you persecute me?" 5 He asked, "Who are you, Lord?" The reply came, "I am Jesus, whom you are persecuting. 6 But get up and enter the city, and you will be told what you are to do." 7 The men who were traveling with him stood speechless because they heard the voice but saw no one. 8 Saul got up from the ground, and though his eyes were open, he could see nothing; so they led him by the hand and brought him into Damascus. 9 For three days he was without sight, and neither ate nor drank.

10 Now there was a disciple in Damascus named Ananias. The Lord said to him in a vision, "Ananias." He answered, "Here I am, Lord." 11 The Lord said to him, "Get up and go to the street called Straight, and at the house of Judas

look for a man of Tarsus named Saul. At this moment he is praying, 12 and he has seen in a vision a man named Ananias come in and lay his hands on him so that he might regain his sight." 13 But Ananias answered, "Lord, I have heard from many about this man, how much evil he has done to your saints in Jerusalem; 14 and here he has authority from the chief priests to bind all who invoke your name." 15 But the Lord said to him, "Go, for he is an instrument whom I have chosen to bring my name before Gentiles and kings and before the people of Israel; 16 I myself will show him how much he must suffer for the sake of my name." 17 So Ananias went and entered the house. He laid his hands on Saul and said, "Brother Saul, the Lord Jesus, who appeared to you on your way here, has sent me so that you may regain your sight and be filled with the Holy Spirit." 18 And immediately something like scales fell from his eyes, and his sight was restored. Then he got up and was baptized, 19 and after taking some food, he regained his strength.

For several days he was with the disciples in Damascus, 20 and immediately he began to proclaim Jesus in the synagogues, saying, "He is the Son of God." 21 All who heard him were amazed and said, "Is not this the man who made havoc in Jerusalem among those who invoked this name? And has he not come here for the purpose of bringing them bound before the chief priests?" 22 Saul became increasingly more powerful and confounded the Jews who lived in Damascus by proving that Jesus was the Messiah.

Discussion
Ask the youth:

>What do you think happened to Paul?
>Would you go if you were Ananias?
>Is this proof of Christianity that someone like Paul would convert?

Close in Prayer

Homework
We have now gone through the Gospels and the book of Acts, what other books are in the New Testament? Write them all out.
Take some times with these other books. What are they about? Why do you think people think they are important? Write out some of what you find.
In any of the book after Acts, find the weirdest/funniest/oddest/most confusing story or command you can find. Weirdest New Testament story gets a prize (AND YES YOU CAN USE THE INTERNET). Explain what you found and why it is weird

Faith Diving Day 21
Other New Testament Books
Location: Inside

Opening Prayer

Highs/Lows
Have the youth share a high event (good) and a low event (bad) from the last week.

Going Over The Homework
Ask the youth to get out their homework assignments. Ask them:

> After Acts, what other books are in the New Testament?
> What did you find in the books after Acts?
> Why do you think people think they are important?
> What weird story did you find? Why do you think it is weird?

New Testament Puzzle
Find the clue, solve the clue, and then place all the clues in the right order to win the prize.

Hide clues for each book of the New Testament (Romans-Revelation) around the church (Have multiple copies at each hiding spot). Then have the youth break into teams of two (or three) and find the clues.

Once they have found the clues, have them figure out what Book (or books) of the bible they represent. Then have them place all the books in the right order. First group to finish gets the best prize.

While they are searching for the clues, have a "books of the New Testament" song playing on repeat endlessly. One possible option is "Books of the New Testament" by Wee Sing.

Romans
Clue: The person with the oar in the boat was definitely a man.
Quote: Romans 3:23-24 "For all have sinned and fall short of the glory of God, and are justified by His grace a gift, through the redemption that is in Christ Jesus."

First and Second Corinthians
Clue: You can be the first or second apple CORE thrown INto a box.
Quote: 1 Corinthians 13:4 "Love is patient, love is kind. It does not envy, it does not boast, it is not proud."

Galatians
Clue: It is not so much a book for GUYS as it is for the other gender.
Quote: Galatians 3:28 "There is neither Jew nor Gentile, neither slave nor free, neither male nor female, for you are all one in Christ Jesus."

Ephesians
Clue: It sounds like it should start with an "F," but it is a whole lot more complicated than that.
Quote: Ephesians 2:8 "For it is by grace you have been saved, through faith – and this is not from yourselves, it is the gift of God."

Philippians
Clue: It's a Mickelson, a doctor, a Collins, a Rivers, and a Cheesestake, but not a mon. Definitely not a mon. There's a whole lot more P's in this one.
Quote: Philippians 4:13 "I can do all this through him who gives me strength."

Colossians
Clue: There was a building where the Romans would fight, back in the day, but you have to get rid of the eum for this to help you solve the clue.

Quote: Colossians 1:16 "For in him all things were created: things in heaven and on earth, visible and invisible, whether thrones or powers or rulers or authorities; all things have been created through him and for him."

First and Second Thessalonians
Clue: There is a fancy word for a place to get a hair cut in the middle of the word.
Quote: 1 Thessalonians 5:21 "But test them all; hold on to what is good"

First and Second Timothy
Clue: An Allen, a Burton, a McGraw, or a Cook will do just fine. Well, you'll need two of them, I suppose.
Quote: 1 Timothy 2:1 "I urge, then, first of all, that petitions, prayers, intercession and thanksgiving be made for everyone"

Titus
Clue: If your belt is too TIGHT, you might be in the United States. Is that a bad joke? No, it is a clue you'll need to shorten.
Quote: Titus 1:2 "In the hope of eternal life, which God, who does not lie, promised before the beginning of time."

Philemon
Clue: This word couldn't be any more sour if it tried. Well, I suppose the sour part could have come at the beginning of the word, but no one's perfect.
Quote: Philemon 1:7 "Your love has given me great joy and encouragement, because you, brother, have refreshed the hearts of the Lord's people."

Hebrews
Clue: This word isn't exactly about beer brewing, but once again it definitely has a masculine element.
Quote: Hebrews 11:1 "Now faith is being sure of what we hope for and certain of what we do not see."

James
Clue: They call him the king or the chosen one in basketball, but to me this book will always be about 007.
Quote: James 1:5 "If any of you lacks wisdom, you should ask God, who gives generously to all without finding fault, and it will be given to you."

First and Second Peter
Clue: It could be the size of pea or a single tear, but when you have two of something it will never truly be small.
Quote: 1 Peter 3:15 "But in your hearts revere Christ as Lord. Always be prepared to give an answer to everyone who asks you to give the reason for the hope that you have. But do this with gentleness and respect"

First, Second, and Third John
Clue: Some people use this as another name for a toilet, but that seems like a waste when you could the first or second or third edition of Madden.
Quote: 1 John 1:9 "If we confess our sins, he is faithful and just and will forgive us our sins and purify us from all unrighteousness."

Jude
Clue: If I told you to take a sad song and make it better, would you have any idea what I was talking about? It'd probably just be easier to ask you who is in charge of a court trial and take the G out of their title.
Quote: Jude 1:3 "Dear friends, although I was very eager to write to you about the salvation we share, I felt compelled to write and urge you to contend for the faith that the Lord has once for all entrusted to us, his people."

Revelation
Clue: If you take the word elevation, rearrange it, and add an R onto the front of it, you'd have this book where everything must end.
Quote: Revelation 3:20 "Here I am! I stand at the door and knock. If anyone hears my voice and opens the door, I will

come in and eat with them, and they with me."

Quiz
When they get done, give the first group an award (candy), but then give them the quiz... most right answers without a phone and most right answers without a phone wins (two prizes... and they have to decide which one they will go for).

12 Questions Quiz
1. What do people call the first four books of the New Testament?
2. Who wrote the most books in the New Testament?
3. Which book comes last in the New Testament?
4. What does the word Gospel mean?
5. What Biblical books tell about Jesus' birth?
6. Who baptized Jesus?
7. Who healed Paul?
8. Where was Jesus born?
9. What made the disciples speak in tongues?
10. How did Jesus feed 5000 people?
11. What happened on Easter morning?
12. How many disciples did Jesus have?

After everyone is back and has finished the Bible Picture hunt and the quiz... Go over the answers to the quiz
Gospels
Paul (or Saul)
Revelation (no S)
Good News
Matthew and Luke
John
Ananias
Bethlehem
The Holy Spirit
Multiplies Fish and Bread
Jesus came back from the dead
12

Bible Walkthrough
Then walk the youth through the different books of the Bible, having them turn their Bibles along as they go. Call out anything of interest you might know or find for each book as you go along. Ask them:

> Why read these books?
> Why do people take the Bible so seriously?
> Do you take the Bible seriously?
> Why read the same stories over and over again?

Close in Prayer

Homework
Think about or look up on the internet arguments FOR and AGAINST Christianity. Come ready to debate either side.

Faith Diving Day 22
Christianity vs. Not-Christianity Debate
Location: Inside

Opening Prayer

Highs/Lows
Have the youth share a high event (good) and a low event (bad) from the last week.

Going Over The Homework
Ask the youth to get out their homework assignments. Ask them:

> In your internet searches did you find any good arguments against Christianity?
> In your internet searches did you find any good arguments for Christianity?

Debate Team
Divide the youth into teams... one for Christianity, one against Christianity. They are going to have a debate. They will have an opening statement. Each side will get a chance to make three points and the other side will get a rebuttal. They will have a closing statement. Adults will judge.

Give them time to divide up the roles and craft their argument... they need to make sure that everyone is involved. They can ask for help in coming up with their arguments. Do not give them all the reasons below, but offer some of them up if they need help. Inform them that the winning team gets a massive prize... Like a pie or something.

Reasons People Don't Believe in Christianity
> The story doesn't make sense, why would God have to die in order to pay for sins to... himself.
> Jesus has not returned, it has been 2000 years.

So many other religions, they could all be true.
There is no soul, we are just physical beings.
Evil exists in the world, a loving God wouldn't allow that.
The bible is not consistent.
The Gospels are not historically reliable.

Reasons People Do Believe in Christianity

Many of the religious texts are surprisingly trustworthy. We have historical and biographical texts that usually would have been written at a much later date.
The way Jesus was found missing (by women) would not be the way you would tell that story if you were making it up.
Jesus appeared to his disciples that had disbanded, had renounced him, and then they came back together and were all martyred for their faith. What else would explain their change?
The continuation of miracles today.
Jesus as a person worthy of praise.

Debate Debrief

After the debate... Ask the youth who they think was the winner. Then let the adults inform them who they think was the winner (obviously Christianity... and adults give testimony about why they are a Christian).

Then inform the youth that anyone that brings up the best reason, in their opinion, for becoming a Christian gets part of the prize. Ask them:

What was it like arguing against Christianity? Did it feel weird? Do you ask some of those same questions?
What was it like defending Christianity? Have you had to do that before? What was that like?
Why do you think we spent time doing this?

Talk to an Adult
After the debate have the youth pair off with adults and ask them why they are Christians.

Close in Prayer

Homework
Below you will find one of our Creeds: The Apostles' Creed. A Creed is a statement of what we believe together. For Next time, try to write out specifically what you believe... be honest. You can use as much or as little of the Apostles' Creed as you want... but don't just copy it, make sure that you make it your own. (AND ALSO... note any confusion you have about the Apostles Creed)

APOSTLES' CREED
I believe in God, the Father almighty, creator of heaven and earth.

I believe in Jesus Christ, God's only Son, our Lord, who was conceived by the Holy Spirit, born of the virgin Mary, suffered under Pontius Pilate, was crucified, died, and was buried; he descended to the dead.* On the third day he rose again; he ascended into heaven, he is seated at the right hand of the Father, and he will come to judge the living and the dead.

I believe in the Holy Spirit, the holy catholic Church, the communion of saints, the forgiveness of sins, the resurrection of the body, and the life everlasting. Amen.

*Or, "he descended into hell."

Faith Diving Day 23
Apostle's Creed
Location: Inside

Opening Prayer

Highs/Lows
Have the youth share a high event (good) and a low event (bad) from the last week.

Going Over The Homework
Ask the youth to get out their homework assignments. Ask them to share their Creeds and questions about the Creed with the group.

For those that didn't do their homework... give them an opportunity to write out something.

Team Creed
Break into teams where you divide up the different parts of the Creed. Depending on Groups and sizes, have them taken portions of the creed.

Have them define what they think their part of the creed is saying, where it is talked about in the Bible (they can use the internet), and whether or not their group believes that part of the creed. Best (most complete) answers win candy.

1. I believe in God, the Father almighty, creator of heaven and earth.
2. I believe in Jesus Christ, God's only Son, our Lord,
3. Who was conceived by the Holy Spirit, born of the virgin Mary,
4. Suffered under Pontius Pilate, was crucified, died, and was buried;
5. He descended to the dead. (Or, "he descended into hell," another translation of this text in widespread use.)
6. On the third day he rose again;

7. He ascended into heaven,
8. He is seated at the right hand of the Father, and he will come to judge the living and the dead.
9. I believe in the Holy Spirit,
10. The holy catholic Church,
11. The communion of saints,
12. The forgiveness of sins,
13. The resurrection of the body, and the life everlasting. Amen.

Have the youth come back and present their part of the creed. Ask them:

> What is the hardest part of the Creed for you (understanding/believing)?
> Why have a Creed if not everyone can agree to it?
> Should we change or update the Creed?
> Is religion a more personal thing (Personal relationship with God) or a shared thing (we worship together)?
> Why worship together?

When Two or Three
Share with the youth the Matthew 18:20 passage (NRSV) "For where two or three are gathered in my name, I am there among them." Let the youth know that we have been promised that God speaks through our neighbor and works through them. If we do it alone... we only have our own resources, but with a group... God has many voices and faces and hands to work through.

Back to Back Game
Play Back to Back Game (if there is time) as a way of showing how we support one another.

This is the game where you start out with two people sitting back to back and they have to stand straight up without using their hands.

Close in Prayer

Homework
Below you will find the Lord's Prayer. It is the prayer that Jesus gave us. For Next time, write out an "all encompassing" prayer to God. You can use as much or as little of the Lord's Prayer as you want… but don't just copy it, make sure that you make it your own. (AND ALSO… note any confusion you have about the Lord's Prayer)

LORD'S PRAYER
Our Father who art in heaven,
Hallowed be thy Name.
Thy kingdom come.
Thy will be done,
On earth as it is in heaven.
Give us this day our daily bread.
And forgive us our trespasses,
As we forgive those who trespass against us.
And lead us not into temptation,
But deliver us from evil.
For thine is the kingdom,
and the power, and the glory,
for ever and ever.

**** And for a bonus prize… find where this is in the New Testament… and see if it is different from what you are used to.

Faith Diving Day 24
Lord's Prayer Scavenger Hunt
Location: Inside

Opening Prayer

Highs/Lows
Have the youth share a high event (good) and a low event (bad) from the last week.

Going Over The Homework
Ask the youth to get out their homework assignments. Ask them to share their Lord's Prayer versions. Also see if anyone found where the Lord's Prayer is in the Bible.

Traditional Lord's Prayer
Our Father who art in heaven,
Hallowed be thy Name.
Thy kingdom come.
Thy will be done,
On earth as it is in heaven.
Give us this day our daily bread.
And forgive us our trespasses,
As we forgive those who trespass against us.
And lead us not into temptation,
But deliver us from evil.
For thine is the kingdom,
and the power, and the glory,
for ever and ever.

Matthew 6:9-13 NRSV version
9 "This, then, is how you should pray: "'Our Father in heaven, hallowed be your name, 10 your kingdom come, your will be done, on earth as it is in heaven. 11 Give us today our daily bread. 12 And forgive us our debts, as we also have forgiven our debtors. 13 And lead us not into temptation, but deliver us from the evil one.'

Ask them:
> Why are there differences?
> What are the differences?
> Why is it important to pray?

Lord's Prayer Scavenger Hunt
Inform the group that you are going to go on an inside the church scavenger hunt and they will need to take a lot of pictures in order to win. They have to follow clues relating to the Lord's Prayer.

The Lord's Prayer begins with
Our Father who art in heaven, hallowed be thy name.
In this beginning of this prayer we say that God is our creator and we must always remember where we come from. Each church has a first pastor... do you know who the first pastor of your church was? They probably have a picture hanging in this church... write down their name and take a picture of their picture.

> Name:
> Picture: Yes No

The Lord's Prayer continues
Thy kingdom come. Thy will be done, on earth as it is in heaven.
In this we are talking about God's reality becoming our reality. We know that the world is a hard place, but we want the world to start looking more like how God intended for it to be... like in a garden...where people in their small community were given direct help from God. Does this church have a community garden? What is it's name? Take a picture by the sign. (If the church doesn't have a community garden, take a picture of where you keep the lawn mower or even just a nicely cared for part of the church property.

> Name:
> Picture: Yes No

The Lord's Prayer continues
Give us this day our daily bread.
Daily bread is not just about food, it is about having everything that we need. And a need is very different from a want. What do you really need? Food, Water, Clothes, Shelter. At this church we take daily bread seriously... do you know we run an evening meal program at this church? What is its name? Take a picture by their food pantry. (If the church doesn't have a feeding program, consider bins where you collect food, or think up other creative options)

    Name:
    Picture: Yes No

The Lord's Prayer continues
And forgive us our trespasses, as we forgive those who trespass against us.
This is about understanding that everyone makes a mistake, that no one is perfect, and because we want forgiveness when we screw up, we must also forgive others. Do you know why we receive forgiveness? It is because of something God did for us... can you think of a place in the church where all that we have done wrong was washed away? Take a picture with that special item in the church sanctuary (the Baptismal font)

    What is this talking about?
    Picture: Yes No

The Lord's Prayer continues
And lead us not into temptation.
This part of the prayer is about the fact that people don't usually do bad because they want to do bad things, but because temptations are very real... and we pray that God will help us to remain focused on better things than the short term enjoyment that comes from giving into our temptations. One temptation that people struggle with is

alcohol. The Lutheran church doesn't think that people shouldn't drink, but we do know that for some it is a real temptation and we do our best to support them. So for communion we serve both wine and grape juice. Can you find where we keep our wine and grape juice? Take a picture with the refrigerator. Bonus point if you learn the name for the room where we keep our wine and grape juice.

    Name of the room
    Picture: Yes No

The Lord's Prayer continues
But deliver us from evil.
There are forces at work in this world that are bigger than we will ever understand. But we know, that we have a protector... one that can and has delivered us from evil. This protector is Jesus, who accomplished all on the cross. See how many crosses you can find in the church, you can get a point for every cross picture you take.

    Picture: Yes No (How Many ___)

The Lord's Prayer continues
For thine is the kingdom.
This world is God's kingdom and we simply live in it. But even though we live in God's kingdom... we still have to have earthly leaders... people in charge. Go take a picture with the picture of the earthly leader of the church. Write down the name of the earthly leader. HINT: This is a trick question. (It should be a picture with the council president)

    Name:
    Picture: Yes No

The Lord's Prayer continues
And the power.
God has real power, God is in complete control. But even

though we have been given God's power... we still need earthly power. Find out where an electrical panel is at the church.

> Picture: Yes No

The Lord's Prayer continues
And the glory.
We like to crown people with glory, but God is really the only one that deserves glory. Do you know God gave us a reminder of God's glory. It hangs in the sky when it rains and there is sunlight. God put it in place after God saved God's people in Noah's Ark. See if you can find a picture of a rainbow in the church. (If there are no rainbows or even picture bible's in the church, have them take a picture outside toward the sun... but don't stare into it!)

> Picture: Yes No

The Lord's Prayer concludes
Forever and ever.
God's kingdom and power and glory with go on forever and ever and ever. Do you know how long forever is? Well... its forever! It is hard for us to imagine what forever looks like, because we are so focused on time... and even though we at the church know God is timeless... we still have a lot of clocks. Take a picture of as many clocks as you can find in the church... get a point for every clock picture.

> How many Pictures?

Debrief
Ask the youth:

> Did anything new stick out to you about the Lord's Prayer?
> Do you think you'll use it regularly to help you pray?

Close in Prayer

Homework
What other Christian denominations are out there (Like Lutheran or Episcopalian) How many can you come up with? Special prize to the person that finds the most.

Faith Diving Day 25
History Of Christianity/Other Denominations
Location: Inside

Opening Prayer

Highs/Lows
Have the youth share a high event (good) and a low event (bad) from the last week.

History of Christianity
Show a brief video on the history of Christianity (one option): https://youtu.be/qlogMDTYeA4

Ask them:

> Is it important to know where we, as a religious tradition, came from?
> What did you just learn (if anything) about our Christian history?
> What do you know about different Christian traditions?

ELCA (Lutherans) and Others
Show video on the difference between the ELCA and Others (one option): https://youtu.be/18PI9bG73o4

Ask them:

> What have you heard about any of the denominations mentioned in the video?
> Does it matter to you (at all) that you go to an ELCA church vs. one of the other options?
> What is a denomination?

Going Over The Homework
Ask the youth what denominations they found. If you have a whiteboard, put the names they come up with up on that. Make sure you include: Catholicism,

Protestantism, Baptists, Lutherans, Presbyterians, Methodists, Pentecostals, Seventh Day Adventists, Episcopalians, Non Denominationals, (Make sure to include whichever Church you will visit next class)

Guess a Denomination
The youth can guess at any time, but after they guess, they can't guess again. First one to get the right response gets candy.

Who Am I?
I am the largest Christian denomination by about 400 million… Sometimes all people talk about is the fact that the pope is the head of this tradition. The one in our area is called (Name of your local Catholic Church). Catholicism - 1.2 billion

Difference between Catholicism and Lutheranism[8]
1. Bible alone. Lutherans believe that the Bible alone has authority to say what we believe; the Catholic Church gives this authority also to the pope, the church, and certain traditions of the church.

2. Grace, grace, grace. Lutherans believe that a person is saved by God's grace, that we are saved because God loves us. The Catholic Church, while at times using similar language, still officially holds that faith, in order to save, must be accompanied by (or "infused with") some "work" or "love" active within a Christian. You have to earn it.

3. No Pope for you. Unlike the Catholic Church, Lutherans do not believe that the pope is appointed by God or that we should follow him.

4. Mary. Unlike Catholics, Lutherans do not believe it is necessary to offer prayers to saints or to Mary the mother

---

[8] https://www.faithlutherancorning.org/lutheran-vs-catholic

of Jesus.

5. Sacraments. Lutherans have only two sacraments (Baptism and communion), while Catholics have more.

Who Am I?
We broke away from the catholic church in the 1500's. We are not one group that broke away, but a collection of some of the churches that broke away. You could say we were protesting Catholicism, but it was much more than that. Protestantism - 800 million

The next group are denominations that fall under protestantism.

Who Am I?
You could say we are followers of John, but that wouldn't be right. You could say we are all about babies in water, but that wouldn't be right either. John was called John the Baptist, and we do wonder if Babies should be baptized, but Baptism is not all there is to us. Our church in your area is called (Name of local baptist church). Baptist churches - 75-105 million

Difference between Baptists and Lutherans
The major differences between Baptists and Lutherans have to do with what the Bible teaches about Baptism and Communion.
1. No Baby Baptism. Baptists believe that a person receiving baptism has to know what they are getting into, and since babies can't really communicate, they cannot receive baptism. Lutherans believe there is no way we could ever understand what is happening in Baptism, and that baptism is not about what you do during Baptism, it is about what God is doing... which means: ANYONE CAN GET BAPTIZED.

2. Communion isn't "real" for Baptists. From Baptists, communion is more of a "commemorative meal" rather

than something where God literally becomes present in the bread and the wine. Lutherans think that because Jesus said that communion is his body and blood... he meant it. God is present at the table.

3. The choice. Baptists believe that people choose God or find God... but Lutherans believe that God finds us.

Who Am I?
I am you and you are me. You could say we are so 500 years ago, but we like to see ourselves as always being made new or always reforming. Some think we started with nailing a piece of paper to a door, but we were attempting to get back to the faith that was there from the beginning. Martin Luther played a big role in getting us started, but we have grown quite a bit since then. Lutheranism - 65-90 million

We will spend quite a bit of time later looking at what exactly "being Lutheran" means.

Who am I?
My name literally means elder in Greek... do you know your Greek? Me neither. You could say that I am the president of churches, but we just share our first four letters. Our church in your area is called (Name of local Presbyterian Church). Presbyterianism - 40-50 million

Difference between Presbyterians and Lutherans
1. Presbyterian churches tend to emphasize the power and glory of God as the central teaching of the Bible, while Lutherans believe that the central teaching of the Bible is grace. God loves us even though we don't deserve it.

2. Lutherans say Jesus died on the cross for everyone, but Presbyterians have a "limited atonement" of Christ, which means that Jesus only died for "the elect"--those who have been predestined from eternity to believe in

Christ and will spend eternity with Him in heaven.

3. Ever heard "damned if you do, damned if you don't?" Most Presbyterian churches teach a "double predestination," which means that some people are predestined by God to be saved and others are predestined by God to hell. That is... it doesn't matter what they do in life, God has chosen from the beginning who is "in" and who is "out". Lutherans... disagree. God loves and "chooses" everyone.

Who am I?
You could say there is a method to my madness and you would be right. You have probably never heard of the trilateral or the quadrilateral of faith... and that is probably for the best. Our church in this area is (Name of Local Methodist church). Methodism - 30-80 million

Differences between Methodists and Lutherans[9]
The primary differences between Lutheranism and "classical" Methodism rooted in the theology of John Wesley center in Wesley's understanding of salvation. Wesley taught, contrary to Lutheran theology, that
1) it is possible for a person to save themselves by making the right choice... Lutherans say God does the work;

2) the Holy Spirit assures humans of their salvation directly, through an inner "experience"... Lutherans say it is not about how you feel, but how much God loves everyone;

3) Christians in this life are capable of Christian perfection and are commanded by God to pursue it (full salvation)... Lutherans would say we are never going to be perfect, but God loves us anyway. Wesley also held to a "symbolic" view of the sacraments in contrast to the Lutheran view

---

[9] https://www.faithlutherancorning.org/lutheran-vs-wesleyan

of the sacraments as real and powerful, with God fully present in them.

Who am I?
I can talk in tongues... can you? This means I can speak a language I have never spoken before and someone else with a special gift can understand it. Pretty cool, huh? The downside... our services tend to last about three hours. There are lots of shouts of Amen, and preach on sister throughout the service, but yeah... they can be a little bit long. Our name comes from the time the Holy Spirit first came on the disciples, just after Jesus passed away. It is also a day in the church year that people refer to as the birthday of the church and NO it is not Christmas. Our church in your area is called (Name of local Pentecostal Church) - 280 million

Differences between Pentecostals and Lutherans[10]
Perhaps the main difference between Lutherans and Pentecostal churches is that Pentecostal churches tend to emphasize the importance of personal and spiritual "experiences" (such as "baptism in the Holy Spirit" and speaking in tongues), while the Lutherans emphasizes the importance and centrality of God's grace and that God has "done everything for you all ready", which remain true and valid regardless of our personal "feelings" or "experiences."

Who Am I?
In case you didn't know, you've got your worship days wrong. Church should be on Saturday and not on Sunday. You should also be vegetarians because eating meat breaks one of the ten commandments... "You shall not kill." The number seven is important to us, probably because it is in our name. Our church in your area is called the (Name of local Seventh-day Adventist Church). Seventh-day Adventist Church - 17 million

---

[10] https://faith-lutheran-church.com/why-lcms%3F

Differences between Seventh-day Adventists and Lutherans
1. Seventh-day Adventists believe that worship should be on Saturday and that worshipping on Saturday is the only way to follow the commandment of "keeping the Sabbath holy." Lutherans would say... you are telling me that even though all christians have been worshipping on Sunday for 1900 years... we were all doing it wrong and will be judged because of it? Early Christians couldn't worship in the Temple on Saturday because they were not allowed in... and Jesus came back on a Sunday.

2. According to Seventh Day Adventists, thou shall not kill must also refer to animals. Meat, although tasty... is murder. Lutherans like meat, can eat meat if they want to, but no meat is okay too... if that's your thing.

3. Seventh-day Adventists look forward to Christ returning soon. Lutherans tend to focus on when Jesus said, "But concerning that day and hour no one knows, not even the angels of heaven, nor the Son, but the Father only" (Matthew 24:36 NRSV). When the end comes... no one knows.

Who am I?
I like my tea, but that is not all there is to me. Some call us stuffy, but we think of ourselves as more stylish, more full of tradition, with one heck of a wardrobe. We were once and still are known as the official church of England, but we are in other countries as well. If you call us the anglo-saxon church you wouldn't be far off. In England we are also known as Anglicans... but in the United States we have a different name. Our church in your ares is (Name of local Episcopalian church). Episcopalians (Anglicans) - 85 million

Differences between Episcopalians and Lutherans[11]

Episcopalians attach great importance to the theory of the apostolic succession. They insist that the apostles (those who knew Jesus firsthand) ordained bishops, these in turn ordained their successors, and so down through the centuries, so that the present-day bishops are the successors of the apostles through an unbroken chain. Scripture knows nothing of such a theory. Episcopalians hold that only bishops who have received their authority in this way can properly ordain ministers and that without such Episcopal ordination a minister cannot validly perform the sacraments. HOWEVER, Lutherans are now in full partnership with the Episcopalian church… so whether their theory of "Apostolic succession" is right or not… we are good… because we have it now too.

Ask them:

> What do you make of all these different traditions?
> How do you know which one is right?
> What do you think Jesus/God thinks about the fact that there are so many churches?
> What do you think the church service will be like when we go to (name of church you will visit at your next meeting)? How do you think it will be different? How will it be the same?
> What is important to you about church? For example, what, if changed about church, would make you very unhappy? What "has to be there" for it to be church?

Hidden Hymnal

Hide hymnals all over the church for the youth to find. Tell the youth to find one and bring it back to our room.

---

[11] https://www.faithlutherancorning.org/lutheran-vs-episcopal

Once you are back in the room, find where the book says how worship is supposed to go (order of worship).

Ask them:

> What do we do vs what does it say we are supposed to do in the hymnal?

Go through the order of worship and talk about the differences. Try to get them to note more of what should be there.

Close in Prayer

Faith Diving Day 26
Attend a Non-Lutheran Service
Location: Another Church

Start by meeting at the church

Opening Prayer

Highs/Lows
Have the youth share a high event (good) and a low event (bad) from the last week.

Church Visit
Arrange with a local church leader to come and visit. If possible try to schedule some time for the students to talk with the church leader after the service.

Before you Leave
Remind kids about being courteous and respectful. Let parents know when you will return.

Debrief Back at the Church
When you get back to the church, if there's time, ask them:

> What was different at that church vs. our church?
> Why do you think they worship the way that they do?
> Is there anything we can learn from how they worship?
> Do you think they are worshipping our God or another God or no God?

Close in Prayer

Homework
Think about what the perfect church service would look like. Start to write out some ideas.

Faith Diving Day 27
Plan Perfect Christian Event
Location: Inside

Opening Prayer

Highs/Lows
Have the youth share a high event (good) and a low event (bad) from the last week.

Christian? Religious?
Ask them:

> What makes something Christian?
> What makes something not Christian?
> What makes something religious?
> What makes something not religious?
> What should Christians do when they get together?
> Why do Christians have church worship services?
> Do you enjoy going to Christian worship services?

Christian Worship Videos
Watch some videos that speak about different Christian worship types. Some possibilities are:
Three types of Christian worship: https://youtu.be/qOGISQIMUSA
Different worship styles: https://youtu.be/WIT6snEMRkM

Ask them:

> Did you connect with anything in those videos?
> What is a church?
> Is there a wrong way to do Christian worship?
> How would you fix how we do church?

The Church
Watch a video about what it means to be a church. One possibility is:
What is a church: https://youtu.be/ifnJtkAnBq4

Planning and Leading the Perfect Event

Have the youth plan the perfect 5 minute Christian event. Do not say service because it doesn't have to be a traditional service, but they need to make the event something that they think Christians WOULD WANT TO GO TO.

They will need to plan it out on their own. It must feature at least some speaking time by them of what they think is important for Christians to hear.

After they are done planning they will be given time to have someone else help them with their Christian event... if they need someone to help with a skit or with lighting candles or whatever help they would need during their event. If their event features food, just pretend you have the food.

So they plan it on their own, but they can have help leading it. Each person will put on a 5 minute perfect Christian event followed by an explanation of why they would go to the event they created and the best event/explanation wins a big prize.

Afterward

Ask them:

> Would you have attended any of those events? Why or why not?
> What is important to you about Christianity? Your faith?
> Does Confirmation/Faith Diving fit into any of this?
> What Christian thing can you do outside of a church?

Close in Prayer

Homework
Within the next week, think about something the faith diving group could do to live out their faith in the local community. Email/text/bring the idea to the leader and one of the ideas will be what the group does for their next Faith Diving time.

Make sure they explain how what they are talking about doing is related to their faith and it cannot be done inside or near the church building.

Faith Diving Day 28
Outreach activity
Location: Outside

Start by meeting at the church

Opening Prayer

Highs/Lows
Have the youth share a high event (good) and a low event (bad) from the last week.

Outreach
Run through the various ideas that were suggested by group. Make sure to touch on the positives of the ideas. Explain why you chose the one that you did and make sure to focus on why you think the outreach event you chose is something a Christian should be doing. Ask them:

> What is the difference between a worship event at church and gathering with other Christians to serve out in the community?
> Do we need to do good deeds like we are going to do in order to get into heaven?

Go do whatever it is you planned to do.

Debrief
Check with the youth to see what they found meaningful, if anything, about your chosen outreach event. See if they want to do something like that again. Consider making plans to do it again if they seem excited about the event.

Homework
Think about topics that are hard to talk about, things we call "hot button" issues. What issues in our society are the hardest for you to talk about or understand? Write down some initial thoughts on those issues.

Faith Diving Day 29
Hot Button
Location: Inside

Opening Prayer

Highs/Lows
Have the youth share a high event (good) and a low event (bad) from the last week.

Going Over The Homework
Ask the youth to get out their homework assignments. Ask them:
> What issues did you write down that are the hardest for you to talk about or understand?

Hot Button Issues Game
Play a modified version of hot potato. Get the kids into a circle and have them pass around a modified soccer ball. Tape various hot button topics onto the different pentagons/hexagons. Each time they catch the ball they have to call out the hot button topic they see first and then they have to pass on the ball without dropping it. Whenever time runs out or someone drops the ball, the person that did not get a chance to pass on the ball has to be the first to say their thoughts about the hot button issue that was last called out.

Before you begin, make sure they understand what each hot button topic means. Let them know that answers to these topics are not to be shared outside the group so people feel they have the freedom to share. Let them know that many of the topics they will get into today have deep meaning for many people within the group and they need to work to be respectful.

Feel free to add the issues you would like your group to talk about, but here are some potential discussion topics:

Suicide
LGBTQIA
Premarital Sex
Abortion
Racism
Gender Equality
Bullying
Drugs and Alcohol
Gun Control
War
Immigration
Euthanasia
Death Penalty
Environmentalism

Debrief
Have the youth talk about their experience of the game and what it was like to talk about those hard things. See if there were any issues they wished the group had talked about. Take the time to talk about those.

Close in Prayer

Homework
Think about your big questions about God, reasons you struggle to believe in God, or any confusions you might have. Try to stump the Faith Diving leader with your odd and ridiculous questions!

Faith Diving Day 30
Big Questions
Location: Inside

Opening Prayer

Highs/Lows
Have the youth share a high event (good) and a low event (bad) from the last week.

Going Over The Homework
Ask the youth to get out their homework assignments. Ask them:
> What are your big questions about God, reasons you struggle to believe in God, or any confusions you have?
> Did you come up with any odd or ridiculous questions to stump your Faith Diving leader?

Big Questions
Hopefully they will come up with enough questions organically so that you don't have to make use of the below list, but try to prompt them to ask their own questions.

> What makes Christianity, Christianity? What is difficult about being a Christian?
> Is Baptism necessary? What about those who don't get Baptized?
> Is Communion really the body and blood of Jesus? Are you okay eating and drinking that?
> What's the hardest part of the Jesus story for you to believe?
> What about other religions/denominations? How do we know who is right?
> Heaven/Hell? Are they real? Who goes to Heaven? Who goes to Hell?
> Do you really have a Holy Spirit within you? Shouldn't you make the right decision more often?

How do we know we can trust what is in the Bible?
Can the Bible tell the future?
Is going to church really important?
Should we even have churches?
Shouldn't we just sleep in on Sundays and talk to God later?
What should churches be doing with their time?
Will you go to church when you or older?
Why do bad things happen to good people?
If God is so perfect, then why did God create something so imperfect allowing pain, suffering and daily atrocities?
How can someone be God's son and God at the same time?
Couldn't God have "saved" us another way than the cross?
Why doesn't God heal more people?
Why do some prayers seem to go unanswered?
Why doesn't God speak to us more clearly?
Why doesn't God just show himself to everyone at once so that everyone can believe?
If God created everything, why did God allow for AIDS, covid, cancer, and every other terrible thing?

Faith Letters

If confirmation day is approaching, talk to "graduating" youth about their faith letters. All the graduating Faith Divers are to write a letter to present on the Sunday of their graduation. Invite them to be open and honest about where their faith is at and where they think it is going.

Have them email these letters to you (the leader) to read and, no matter what, prompt them to say a little more and push them to be even more honest. They know what we want them to say, but we want to actually hear where they are.

Faith Diving, Confirmation Ritual
Explain to the graduating youth what sort of ritual your church uses for confirmation so they are prepared. Also, make sure to remind them that they are welcome to continue with faith diving.

For kids not graduating... two weeks after the graduation we will go see as "religious" a movie as we can find in theaters.

Close in Prayer

Homework
For the graduates, their homework is their faith letter. For the non-graduates encourage them to think about how we can learn about God, not just from religious things, but also from nearly anything... including a big box office movie that on the surface has almost nothing to do with God.

Faith Diving Day 31
Faith Diver Graduation
Location: Church

Faith Letter
All the Faith Divers are to write a letter to read in front of the church on the Sunday of their graduation. Invite them to be open and honest about where their faith is at and where they think it is going. At my church we have this faith diving sharing moment as the sermon for the day.

For youth who have a strong fear of speaking in public we have them record a video to share with the congregation.

Ritual
After the Faith Diver Faith Letter sharing time, hold whatever "Affirmation of Faith" ritual your church is accustomed to using.

Faith Diving Day 32
Movie for non-graduates
Location: Movie Theatre

Meet at the church

Opening Prayer

Highs/Lows
Have the youth share a high event (good) and a low event (bad) from the last week.

Before Movie Conversation
Ask the youth:
> What are they hoping to learn more about next year?
> What helped them this year to learn more about their faith?
> What confused them this year?

Go See a Movie
It can be a faith based movie if one is available, but can be anything. Make sure you debrief after the movie is over.

Close in Prayer

End Year 2

Year 3
Lutheranism and Other Religions

Faith Diving Day 33
Watch Luther Movie Part 1
Location: Inside Church

Opening Prayer

Highs/Lows
Have the youth share a high event (good) and a low event (bad) from the last week.

Welcome in the New Class.
Welcome the returning students. Explain the nature of faith diving.

Lutheran Discussion
Ask them:

> What does it mean to be Lutheran?
> Is there something that is particularly Lutheran?
> Does it matter whether or not you are Lutheran?
> Do you know any famous Lutherans?

Famous Lutherans?
Watch this Lost and Found video:
https://www.youtube.com/watch?v=1O2kvQ1dWoY

Ask them:

> Does it matter to you if famous or "intelligent" or "successful" people believe something or not?
> Does it make sometime more appealing if you know someone else that does it or is part of it?

Introduction to Martin Luther
Ask them:

What have you heard about Martin Luther?

Luther Movie Part 1
Watch the first 23 minutes of the Luther Movie starring Joseph Fiennes. A link to the movie can be found here: https://www.amazon.com/Luther-Joseph-Fiennes/dp/B001EMYRHU

Watch from opening credits to just before the Communion after the suicide in Wittenberg.

Areas to focus on with Comments:

Thrivent Logo
Comment on the Thrivent financial for Lutherans logo… talk about Lutheran presence around the world during titles… Lutheran World Relief, other Lutheran organizations you are aware of.

Luther on the Road
Talk about Luther's response to fear… try to explain what he is doing on the road.

Penitent Man on the Ground
Talk about old forms of receiving forgiveness. That it was not as simple as telling God you were sorry. Forgiveness was hard to come by in Luther's time.

Opening Communion
How is what he is doing with worship different than what your church does for worship?

Sweating Luther
Why is he sweating? Talk about how Luther struggled with fear, among other things.

Languages of that time period
What language is he speaking? What was his everyday language?

Luther with his father
Explain father scene. Explain that Luther's father wanted him to be a lawyer, which he had agreed to do until lightening made him vow to become a monk.

Sin With Abbot and Luther
Too full of sin? What could that mean? Ask the youth What sin is to them? What does sin do? Do you believe God keeps track of your sins?

Merciful God
Luther was looking for a merciful God... what does it mean for God to be merciful? Ask youth if they think God is merciful, loving, compassionate? How would they react if they were told God is not those things?

Rome/Holy Objects/Indulgences
Rome as a holy place. People purchasing Holy objects for protection or other benefits. Asks the youth if they think certain items can be more holy than others? Explain indulgences, the purchasing of forgiveness for you or a family member.

Pope in armor
Explain to the youth the level of power and control the church had in those days. That the pope was not just a peaceful leader, but one who could lead an army to war.

Holy Roman Church
In those days it was believed by the Holy Roman

Church that there was no salvation outside of the Holy Roman Church. Ask the youth if they think you have to be part of the right religion/denomination to receive salvation?

Suicide
Ask the youth what they think about suicide and God? How does God feel about it? About those who have committed suicide. Encourage them to share while also acknowledging that this is a very sensitive subject.

Angry God
Ask the youth if they think God is ever angry? Would God get angry at them?

End before communion

Movie Debrief
Ask them:

> Was there anything in the movie that stuck out to you?
> Is there any part of the movie you want to know more about?
> What do you think about Martin Luther as depicted in this movie?

Sanctuary Differences
Go into the church Sanctuary and share with the faith divers that Martin Luther wrote a short book called the Small Catechism in order to teach younger people just like them.

Go to Baptismal Font[12]
Explain to the youth that Martin Luther said that,

---

[12] https://catechism.cph.org/en/sacrament-of-holy-baptism.html

"Baptism is not just plain water, but it is the water included in God's command and combined with God's word. Christ our Lord says in the last chapter of Matthew: 'Therefore go and make disciples of all nations, baptizing them in the name of the Father and of the Son and of the Holy Spirit.' (Matthew 28:19)

"What benefits does Baptism give? It works forgiveness of sins, rescues from death and the devil, and gives eternal salvation to all who believe this, as the words and promises of God declare."

Ask them:

> Do you believe this about baptism?
> Does it matter to you what Martin Luther said about Baptism?

Go to Communion Table[13]
Explain to the youth that Martin Luther said about communion that, "It is the true body and blood of our Lord Jesus Christ under the bread and wine, instituted by Christ Himself for us Christians to eat and to drink. Where is this written? The holy Evangelists Matthew, Mark, Luke, and St. Paul write:Our Lord Jesus Christ, on the night when He was betrayed, took bread, and when He had given thanks, He broke it and gave it to the disciples and said: 'Take, eat; this is My body, which is given for you. This do in remembrance of Me.' In the same way also He took the cup after supper, and when He had given thanks, He gave it to them, saying, 'Drink of it, all of you; this cup is the new testament in My blood, which is shed for you for the forgiveness of sins. This do, as often as you drink it, in remembrance of Me.' These words, 'Given and shed for you for the forgiveness of sins,' show us that in the Sacrament forgiveness of sins, life, and salvation are

---

[13] https://catechism.cph.org/en/sacrament-of-the-altar.html

given us through these words. For where there is forgiveness of sins, there is also life and salvation."

Ask them:

>   Do you believe this about communion?
>   Does it matter to you what Martin Luther said about communion?
>   How much should your being Lutheran influence what you believe?
>   What more do you want to know about Lutheranism?

Close in Prayer

Homework
Write out what you think Baptism and Communion really mean. Try to put into words where you might agree or disagree with Martin Luther.

Faith Diving Day 34
Watch 2nd part of Luther movie/95 Theses
Location: Inside Church

Opening Prayer

Highs/Lows
Have the youth share a high event (good) and a low event (bad) from the last week.

Going Over The Homework
Ask the youth to get out their homework assignments. Ask them:

> What does Baptism mean to you?
> What does Communion mean to you?
> Where do you agree with Martin Luther on Baptism and communion?
> Where do you disagree with Martin Luther on Baptism and communion?

Luther Movie Part 2
Pick back up with the part of the movie where Dr. Luther is teaching and says "Ass."

A link to the movie can be found here:
https://www.amazon.com/Luther-Joseph-Fiennes/dp/B001EMYRHU

Areas to focus on with Comments:

Ass
Ask the youth what they think about proper language in church? Is there a right way to talk in church?

Indulgences
Indulgences.... earning or buying salvation. Ask the youth if you can "cheat" your way into heaven?

Purgatory
What is purgatory (a "temporary" place in between heaven and hell)? Ask the youth if they think such a place exists? Do they believe in heaven and hell? Where would they send kind of bad people?

Prince's Son Talking to Luther
Speaking up even when it might cost you... he might lose his job, his calling, everything to be honest. Ask the youth what costs they see when they are honest? Does God expect them to be honest?

Two Men Walking Up Stairs
Ask the youth what is a pope? Are some people more religious or closer to God than others? What about Christians that do bad things? What does God think of them? Are they further away from God?

Wealth
Ask the youth what they think of churches or religious people that are supposed to be devoted to the poor having all this wealth?

John Teztel
Scaring people straight... Ask the youth what they think of Hell? Is it real? Who goes? How bad is it? Is there hope for people in hell?

Forgiveness
Ask the youth how we get forgiveness?

95 Theses
Nailing the 95 theses to the church. Explain to the youth that this wasn't an act of vandalism, but more of a bulletin board of the day. Explain to

the youth that these 95 theses are seen by many as the beginning of the "Protestant Reformation," as with this document Luther hoped to reform, on a small scale, the things that were wrong with the church.

Printing Press
Explain to the youth that the printing press was a big deal in allowing regular people to have access to ideas they never had before. It was also how Luther's words spread so quickly.

Heretic
Ask the youth what it mean to be a heretic (a person at odds with the expected order)? Ask the youth if they can think of anything that would be considered "heretical" today?

Excommunication
Ask the youth what is excommunication? Should a church kick people out?

Stop before Luther leaves for Rome
Ask the youth why they think Luther didn't keep his big mouth shut? Are we called by God to say certain things?

Movie Debrief
Ask them:

> Was there anything in the movie that stuck out to you?
> Is there any part of the movie you want to know more about?
> What do you think about Martin Luther as depicted in this movie?

95 Theses
Beforehand, make some fancier looking paper by dyeing the paper with tea, or burning parts of it, or making it look old or scroll like.

Have the youth break into groups and write their own "95 Theses" about things that need to change about Christianity today and/or their church. Have them post their documents in a prominent spot.

Close in Prayer

Homework
Find out what a Lutheran Bishop is and what they do (You can look is up online). Write out why you think there might be a need for someone to be in charge of all the pastors and churches? Do you think every church should be able to do whatever it wants? Why or why not? What would you do if you were Bishop?

Faith Diving Day 35
Visit a Bishop
Location: Bishop's Offices

Meet first at the church

Opening Prayer

Highs/Lows
Have the youth share a high event (good) and a low event (bad) from the last week.

Going Over The Homework
Ask the youth to get out their homework assignments. Ask them:

> What is a Lutheran Bishop and what do they do?
> Why might there be a need for someone to be in charge of all the pastors and churches?
> Do you think every church should be able to do whatever it wants? Why or why not?
> What would you do if you were Bishop?

Bishop Visit
Arrange to visit the bishops office to talk with the Bishop about the role of a synod, Lutheranism in general, and allow the kids to ask the bishop tough questions. Prepare the youth to tell the Bishop how they think the church should change.

Debrief
If possible meet with the youth afterward and ask them:

> Did anything stick out to you in your meeting with the Bishop?
> What does it mean to be part of a larger church? Is it important?

Close in Prayer

Homework
Do some research online about Martin Luther. See if you can find any problems that people had with Martin Luther. Try to find the weirdest Luther quote that you can find.

Faith Diving Day 36
Luther's Dark Side/American Lutheranism
Location: Inside Church

Opening Prayer

Highs/Lows
Have the youth share a high event (good) and a low event (bad) from the last week.

Going Over The Homework
Ask the youth to get out their homework assignments. Ask them:

> What did you find out about Martin Luther?
> What problems did people have with Martin Luther?
> What weird Luther quote did you find?

Why Lutheranism?
Watch the a video on why being Lutheran matters. A possible video can be found here: https://youtu.be/TQQaxcadqAQ

Discussion
Ask them:

> Does being Lutheran actually matter anymore?
> Was there anything presented in the video that makes you want to be a Lutheran?
> Why are you a Lutheran?

The Dark Side of Martin Luther
Explain to you the youth that you are going to now talk about a more serious topic, you are going to talk about some of the things Luther said that has no part in any religious tradition, but is something they should probably know about Martin Luther as Lutherans.

Ask them:

> Do you know what it means to be antisemitic? (Anti-Jewish)
> Do you know why some people are antisemitic?
> Would it bother you to hear that Martin Luther, later in life wrote some very antisemitic things?

For more detailed information, read "The Darker Side of Martin Luther" by Emily Paras.[14]

Share with the youth part of what Emily Paras had to say, "Luther's attitude toward the Jews appeared to change over his life. His earlier attitudes seemed were sympathetic towards the Jews. The most convincing evidence of this is his publication in 1523 of the essay That Jesus Christ Was Born a Jew. In it, he urges Christians to treat Jews more gently, and condemns those who treat them as inhuman. Specifically he accuses Catholics of being unfair to them, arguing that,

"'If I had been a Jew and had seen such dolts and blockheads govern and teach the Christian faith, I would sooner have become a hog than a Christian. They have dealt with the Jews as if they were dogs rather than human beings; they have done little else than deride them and seize their property.'

"This quote will stand out later in stark contrast to Luther's later works about the Jews.
He even goes so far as to write, 'If we really want to help them, we must be guided in our dealings with them...we must receive them cordially, and permit them to... hear our Christian teachings and witness our Christian life.'"

---

[14] https://www.iwu.edu/history/constructingthepastvol9/Paras.pdf

But let the youth know that Luther's views soon came to much darker place for, according to Emily Paras, "In 1543 Luther published his infamous On the Jews and Their Lies... Throughout the treatise he decried the Jews, claiming they were 'an idle and lazy people, such a useless, evil, pernicious people, such blasphemous enemies of God.' He especially stressed the commonly held belief during this time that because Jews made their livelihood through usury, they were able to steal and rob from others: 'we let them get rich on our sweat and blood, while we remain poor and they suck the marrow from our bones.' After ranting and raving about the Jews, he gave his advice to his fellow Christians. This advice is in the form of an eight-point plan to deal with the Jews. This plan is most often referred to when scholars attempt to connect Luther with Hitler."

Explain to the youth that this is a truly troubling part of our "founders" thinking and something we can't just ignore, but must be aware of, and work to combat.

Ask them:

> How does this affect your view of Martin Luther?
> How does this affect your views of Lutheranism?

Remind them that Lutheranism is not truly about Martin Luther, but about working to make sure that our faith doesn't remain trapped in the past or trapped by a particular way of thinking, but our protestant faith is about being able to listen for what the Holy Spirit is saying to us now and how we can respond. Lutheranism quickly expanded beyond Martin Luther and Germany.

Lutheranism in the US
Watch a video about the expansion of Lutheranism beyond Germany into the United States. One option is: https://youtu.be/18PI9bG73o4

If you watch the suggested video show 0-1:30 and pause
Ask them:

> Does it truly matter where we came from?
> What do you make of our name... Evangelical Lutheran Church In America?
> Have you heard of other Lutheran groups?

If you watch the suggested video show 1:31-2:51
Ask them:

> Have you heard of the Missouri Synod?
> How should we read the Bible?
> Did all the stories in the Bible happen?
> What do you do with certain difficult Bible passages?
> > Like ones that say women shouldn't speak in public or something about divorce or homosexuality?

Luther Bible Sardines
Talk to the youth about Martin Luther working to translate the Bible not just into German, but common German, a German that everyone could speak. He wanted the Bible to be available for everyone. This game is a take on Sardines. Go hide a Bible somewhere in the church. Tell the youth to go and find the Bible and if they find the Bible they should quietly hide with the Bible. Game goes on until all the youth have found the Bible.

Close in Prayer

Homework
Talk to someone you know that is a Lutheran. Ask them why they are a Lutheran and if being Lutheran is important to them. Encourage them to be honest with you.

Faith Diving Day 37
Talk to a Lutheran/Service Project
Location: Inside Church

Opening Prayer

Highs/Lows
Have the youth share a high event (good) and a low event (bad) from the last week.

Going Over The Homework
Ask the youth:
> Did you talk to someone about why they were Lutheran? What did they say?
> Was being Lutheran important to them? If so, why?

Talk to a Lutheran
Have some older members of the congregation come and talk to the youth about what it means to be Lutheran for them.

The youth will (hopefully) pair off 1:1 with an older adult and ask them four questions (give them a hand out to write on).

Questions
Have the youth ask the adults:

> Have you always been a Lutheran? If so, what was it like growing up Lutheran? If not, what made you come to Lutheranism?
> What is special about being Lutheran? Is being Lutheran better than being another denomination? If so, why? If not, why not?
> Does it still matter today whether you are Lutheran or not?
> What do you wish you knew about faith when you were my age?

Debrief
After they have been given time to discuss (about ten minutes... if the talks are going well do not stop them) invite everyone back to sit around a large table and discuss what they heard.

After youth have shared the answers that they heard (and adults are given a chance to add), ask the adults some follow up questions.

Follow up Questions
Ask them:

> What have you gotten out of your faith? Why is it important to follow God?
> Have you ever experienced a miracle?
> Why are you involved with a church?
> Do you think our faith requires us to help people?

Thank the older members for coming and helping out.

Service Event
If there is extra time have the youth take part in a service event of some kind. Make sure to remind them of all that the Lutheran Church does in the world to help people.

Close in Prayer

Homework
Ask Parents/Grandparents/Guardians what they wanted to be "when they grew up" when they were your age. Then ask what they ended up doing "for a living" and if they were happy with their job. Why/why not?

Faith Diving Day 38
Figure out your calling/Vocation
Location: Inside Church

Opening Prayer

Highs/Lows
Have the youth share a high event (good) and a low event (bad) from the last week.

Going Over The Homework
Ask the youth:

> What did your parents/grandparents/guardians say they wanted to be "when they grew up" when they were your age?
> What do they do now or what did do?
> Were they happy with their job? Why/Why not?

Guess the Job Game
Youth put a piece of paper on their head that has a job on it. They have to guess what their job is by asking other youth yes or no questions. Winner is fastest, although they all get candy if they finish. Probably play twice with two separate sets of cards.

Vocation
Define vocation. A job vs. what you are called to do. That your job "fits" you.

Ask them:

> Do you think God created you with a job/vocation in mind? Does God work like that?
> Is your vocation kind of like the guessing game where everyone else or God knows it before you do?
> Do you have any idea what your vocation or calling might be, "what do you want to do when you grow up?"

Have the youth go off in quiet prayer time where they ask God in their head what God wants them to do with their lives. Have them work on listening to the silence.

After some time, have them write out answers to the following questions. Tell them they have to write something for each question and even if they have no idea about some of them, they have to at least guess. Here are the questions:

> Did you hear anything back from God?
> Do you have a sense of what God wants you to do with your life?
> Do you have a sense of what you want to do with your life?
> Do you think you want to do what God wants you to do?
> Does God make plans for your life?
> Have you ever felt God doing something in your life?
> If God makes plans for you then why do bad things happen?

Debrief
Have the youth share, what they are willing to share. When they have done so, ask them:

> When does a "calling" starts. Does God only expect something of you when you grow up?
> What does God expect you to do right now.

Close in Prayer

Homework
Answer the following questions:
> What is a church?
> What is a church supposed to do? On Sunday? During the Week?
> What should a church never do?

What should people believe in to be a church?
Are all churches the same? What makes them different?
Have you been to other churches? If so what was different about their church from this church?
What do you like about your church?
What do you not like about your church?
What would you do differently?
Have you ever been to a "new" church... one that just started?
Why would someone start a new church?

Faith Diving Day 39
Create Your Own Mission Start
Location: Inside Church

Opening Prayer

Highs/Lows
Have the youth share a high event (good) and a low event (bad) from the last week.

Invite in your local DEM (Director for Evangelical Mission) and have them tell the kids about:

    What a DEM does.
    What is a mission start.
    What mission starts we have in our area.
    Whose job it is to start a mission.
    Who has a calling to share God with other people?

Going Over The Homework
Ask the youth (and make sure the DEM feels comfortable stepping in to help answer some questions):

    What is a church?
    What is a church supposed to do? On Sunday? During the Week?
    What should a church never do?
    What should people believe in to be a church?
    Are all churches the same? What makes them different?
    Have you been to other churches? If so what was different about their church from this church?
    What do you like about your church?
    What do you not like about your church?
    What would you do differently?
    Have you ever been to a "new" church... one that just started?
    Why would someone start a new church?

Mission Start

Now split the group into teams of no more than three, but shoot for groups of two. They have to come up with a plan for a mission start (a new church).

Inform the youth that they have to come up with a plan for a new church that must include:

> Name of New Church and why you named it that way
> Location of New Church and why you located it where you did
> What kind of building or location you will have (Draw plans if necessary)
> What is your Target Audience (who are you trying to attract) and how will they reach them
> How your church be different than every other church
> What will be your worship style, what will your worship services look like
> How will you get the word out about your new church
> How will your new church get money
> How will all ages get involved
> How "Lutheran" would it be

Give them a decent amount of time to put their plan together. Then give them a little more time to think about how they are going to present their Mission start to the DEM (or whoever you can get to judge).

After they have put their plans together have them make a presentation to the DEM and Pastor and whoever else. Best plan gets... something.

Close in Prayer

Homework
(Before every kid leaves, give them a hymnal)
Look through the hymnal and find out what is inside.

Faith Diving Day 40
Different Parts of a Worship Service
Location: Inside Church

Opening Prayer

Highs/Lows
Have the youth share a high event (good) and a low event (bad) from the last week.

Going Over The Homework
Ask the youth:

> Did you look at the hymnal? What was in it?
> Did you know any of the songs?
> Were any of the words familiar?
> What does it mean to be a Lutheran Worship Service?
> Why have a hymnal?
> Why have many churches stopped using a hymnal?
> What has to happen during a church service for it to be a church service in your opinion?
> What should never happen in a church service?

Worship Games
Introduce the idea to the youth that many churches worship in very different ways. What we consider normal, might not be worship at all to someone else. Let them know that they are going to try some different ways of worshipping to show some of those different worship service viewpoints and hopefully have fun.

Praise Jesus
Explain to the youth that as some churches, people regularly shout out things when they feel moved by the Holy Spirit. Invite the youth to attempt to do their most powerful, loudest, shouting of "PRAISE JESUS!"

Fire and Brimstone
Explain to the youth that in some churches the

preacher tries to scare people onto the "right path." These preachers are often referred to as "Fire and Brimstone" preachers as they often spend a great deal of time talking about hell. Invite the youth to the pulpit and have them give their best, short "Fire and Brimstone" sermon.

Liturgical Dance
In some churches people will dance with they feel moved. Some churches even incorporate dance into the service itself, where each dance helps to speak to the theme or message of the day. Let the youth know that this is often referred to as "Liturgical Dance" and invite them to do their best dance around a particular topic.

Baby Baptism Save
Explain to the youth that each church tradition has different ways of doing baptism, from full immersion to just a sprinkling. For this game, they need to catch a baby (Get a toy doll baby) that has slipped out of the pastor's hands during the baptism.

Way Too Long Prayer
In some church people go on and on and on as they pray. Invite the youth to give their best long winded prayer (longest, most boring prayer wins).

Hymnal
Walk them through a worship service setting in the hymnal that your congregation uses or has used in the past. Work to explain as much as you can all the various parts that make up the service.

Plan a Service
Have the youth break into teams and, with the help of a hymnal, invite the youth to create and lead the best worship service.

Give them a hand out that says something like:

> It is now time for you to plan your perfect worship service, how you would do a worship service if you were in charge. You can use a hymnal for inspiration.
>
> Your service must include:
>
> > An order of worship (bulletin/plan)
> > A welcome/introduction to your worship service
> > A Bible Reading (one they find important)
> > A one minute sermon (to be given during presentation) about what a worship service should be.
> > A song (any song that fits... you can find it online)
> > A prayer (or prayers)
> > Something special (Can be anything)
> > A blessing

Have each group put on their worship service, choose a "winner."

Debrief
If you have time, check in with the youth about why they chose what they chose in their service and what each group thinks of the "other" performances and services.

Close in Prayer

Homework
Think about what you would actually change about our worship services, what you would do differently, and how you would do it. Make sure you get specific in your answers because you, with the help of the worship planning team, are going to be in charge of a worship service.

Faith Diving Day 41
Plan A Sunday Worship Service
Location: Inside Church

Opening Prayer

Highs/Lows
Have the youth share a high event (good) and a low event (bad) from the last week.

Going Over The Homework
Before bringing in your special guests, ask the youth:

> What would actually change about our worship services?
> What you would do differently?
> How you would do it differently?

Plan an Upcoming Sunday Service
Bring in everyone that normally helps to plan and lead a worship service including secretary, music leaders, altar guild, ushers, greeters, readers, pastor... anyone that either helps to plan or helps to lead the service itself.

Have the various people that you have invited work to explain how every part of the worship service "happens." Have the regular Sunday bulletins ready to go for them to correct and change.

Explain to the youth that they are going to pick every single part of the worship service, from how the greeters greet people, to the songs, to the readings, to how offering is collected, to how communion is done... every single part of it. Let them know they also have to lead or take part in at least some part of the worship service. For example, if they agree to do the prayer then they write the prayer, or if they agree to do the sermon, have them work with pastor to write the sermon.

Spend the time of the meeting to really plan an upcoming service. Make sure to spend extra time explaining each step of the process.

Close in Prayer

Homework
Everyone's homework is going to be different as they must prepare to lead that next worship service.

Faith Diving Day 42
Run the Worship Service
Location: Inside Church

Before the Service
Opening Prayer

Highs/Lows
Have the youth share a high event (good) and a low event (bad) from the last week.

Check in
Explain to the youth that even though their "job" is to do their part of the worship service, they truly also need to pay special attention to the worship service and the changes they made. Let them know you are going to be asking their opinion about things went.

During the Service
Leaders
Have the youth take part in the service they planned. Consider recording it and watching it with the youth in order to let them think more deeply about why we do the different parts of worship that we do and to evaluate the changes they made.

After the Service
Debrief
Make sure to thank the youth for putting in the work that they did. Spend your time going over what each youth did and the changes they made on the regular service. Ask them to evaluate each part.

Close in Prayer

Homework
Off the top of your head, what religions, do you know about? What does each one you know about believe? Now using the internet, find a new religion that interests you.

Faith Diving Day 43
World Religions Part 1
Location: Inside Church

Opening Prayer

Highs/Lows
Have the youth share a high event (good) and a low event (bad) from the last week.

Going Over The Homework
Ask the youth:
> What religions off the top of your head did you know about? What do they believe?
> What religion, other than Christianity, did you find that interested you? What about them interests you?

Draw God
Give the youth a piece of white paper and something to draw with... tell them to draw God.

After they have completed their drawings, ask them:

> What did you draw and why?
> Does God have a body?
> Does God look the same for everyone?
> Have you ever heard people talk about another God than the God of Christianity?
> Do you think all religions have the same God or are there different ones?

Major Religions Video
Let them know that you are going to watch a Ted Talk on the five major world religions... you can find the link here: https://youtu.be/m6dCxo7t_aE

It is not perfect, and people will disagree on many of the "facts" but it does give a good general introductions into five major religions in our world. Also let them know you will be taking a break after each religion to briefly talk about what they just heard.

Pause after introduction (0-:38)
    What did you think of the intro on religion.
    Do you think we come from a higher power?
    Do you ever wonder about the after life?
    Do you think there are some things that could only be answered by faith or religion?

Pause after Hinduism (:39-2:20)
    What did you think of Hinduism?
    Hinduism is actually much older than what was set out in the video, in fact some of the oldest known writings in existence come from Hinduism... what do you think of the fact that Hinduism has been around longer than Christianity?
    What do you think about reincarnation?
    What do you think of all the different Gods that are actually all one?

Pause after Judaism (2:21-4:20)
    How much of the story of Judaism do you know?
    Do you think there is just one God?
    What connection does Christianity have with Judaism?

Pause after Buddhism (4:21-6:27)
    Why do you think so many things started in India?
    What do you think of miracle birth stories?
    Why must people suffer?
    What does it mean to live a balanced life?

Pause after Christianity (6:28-8.25)
    Did you learn anything new about Christianity?

What do you think of the connections between all these world religions?
Can we learn about Christianity and our own faith from studying these other religions?

Pause after Islam (8.26-10:25)
What have you heard about Islam?
Is Allah the same as our God?
What does it mean to surrender to the will of God?
What do you think about having to pray five times a day every day?

After Conclusion
What did you think of that video?

Close in Prayer

Homework
Talk to your family about what they think about other religions and what they think happens to people that believe in other religions when they die.

Faith Diving Day 44
World Religions Part 2
Location: Inside Church

Opening Prayer

Highs/Lows
Have the youth share a high event (good) and a low event (bad) from the last week.

Going Over The Homework
Ask the youth:

> What did your family say that they think about other religions?
> What did your family say they think happens to people that believe in other religions when they die.
> What do you think about other religions?
> What do you think happens to people from other religions when they die?

Play "Religion" Game
Let the youth know that you are going to have them close their eyes and then you are going to place an object in the middle of the group that they must try to figure out what it is only by touch and without picking it up. Explain that they can't guess what the object was until after everyone has gotten a chance to touch the object.

Now have everyone close their eyes and place a rather large, random object in the middle of the group. After they guess, have them close their eyes again and repeat. Do this a number of times.

After you have played the game a number of times talk to the youth about how sometimes people try to explain the different views of God as coming basically from a bunch of people with their eyes closed feeling around and then those people end up explaining God completely from the piece of God that they have felt. The analogy is usually around an elephant and how people describe the part they are feeling as the whole part... God is an elephant's trunk, God is a leg, God is a belly, God has big ears.

Ask them:

> Do you think this analogy works?
> Do you think this is why we have so many different descriptions and understandings of God?
> Which religion do you think is more "right" about their views on the afterlife?

Afterlife Videos
Have the youth watch a video or videos on various views about the afterlife. Possible options are:

7 Afterlife Views: https://youtu.be/n1p937dkQHQ
Christian views on Afterlife: https://youtu.be/4_bb2etuVzI

Ask the youth:

> What do you think happens when you die?
> Why are there so many different beliefs?
> How do you know which one is the right one?

Close in Prayer

Homework
Bring Something to Be Baptized. Bring your Bible. Bring your favorite kind of bread.

Faith Diving Day 45
What do You Believe?
Location: Inside Church

Opening Prayer

Highs/Lows
Have the youth share a high event (good) and a low event (bad) from the last week.

Wrapping Up
Explain to the youth that this faith diving session is meant to try to tie everything back together after digging into so many different and difficult topics. The goal of this class time is to "re-ground" them in the simple parts of Christianity.

Have the youth write out answer to the following questions:

> What are the most important parts of Christianity?
> What part of what Jesus did is most important, in your opinion?
> What part(s) of Christianity do you find odd?
> What is the hardest thing for you to believe about the Bible/Christian stories?
> What Bible/Christian stories mean the most to you?
> What is Baptism? What is different about a baptized person than a non-baptized person?
> What is communion? What is different about you after you take communion?

Go over their answers.

Baptism
Go and baptize whatever it is they brought with them. Ask them:

> If baptism works how you think it does, what is now different about your item?
> Why do we baptize?
> What does it mean if someone isn't baptized?
> Why do we baptize in the name of the Father Son and Holy Spirit? How can you have three in one?
> Who was/is Jesus?

Act out the Life of Jesus
Break everyone into two groups. Using their Bibles, inform the youth that you'd like them to find what they think are the most important stories of Jesus' life from start to finish and use props to tell, briefly, the full story of who Jesus was. After each scene the youth will need to tell why that scene was so important.

Debrief
Talk about the fact that all of our faith, all of our church, all of our world even comes back around to Jesus, to what we think about Jesus, to what we think Jesus did for us.

Ask the youth:

> What did Jesus do for us?
> Who is Jesus to you?
> Is Jesus still with us?

Communion
Go to the altar and have the youth bring forward their favorite bread. Talk to them about how Jesus made this communion table as a place of comfort, like our favorite bread can be comforting. The communion meal is meant to remind us that no matter how complicated the world might be, we can always come back and find Jesus there, in that communion bread, waiting for us.

Ask the youth:

> Why is communion important as it relates to Jesus?
> What do you think is going on with communion?

Close in Prayer

Homework
Think about topics that are hard to talk about, things we call "hot button" issues. What issues in our society are the hardest for you to talk about or understand? Write down some initial thoughts on those issues and how you think faith/religion should help you to answer those questions.

Faith Diving Day 46
Hot Button
Location: Inside

Opening Prayer

Highs/Lows
Have the youth share a high event (good) and a low event (bad) from the last week.

Going Over The Homework
Ask the youth to get out their homework assignments. Ask them:
> What issues did you write down that are the hardest for you to talk about or understand?

Hot Button Issues Game
Play a modified version of hot potato. Get the kids into a circle and have them pass around a modified soccer ball. Tape various hot button topics onto the different pentagons/hexagons. Each time they catch the ball they have to call out the hot button topic they see first and then they have to pass on the ball without dropping it. Whenever time runs out or someone drops the ball, the person that did not get a chance to pass on the ball has to be the first to say their thoughts about the hot button issue that was last called out.

Before you begin, make sure they understand what each hot button topic means. Let them know that answers to these topics are not to be shared outside the group so people feel they have the freedom to share. Let them know that many of the topics they will get into today have deep meaning for many people within the group and they need to work to be respectful.

Feel free to add the issues you would like your group to talk about, but here are some potential discussion topics:

Suicide
LGBTQIA
Premarital Sex
Abortion
Racism
Gender Equality
Bullying
Drugs and Alcohol
Gun Control
War
Immigration
Euthanasia
Death Penalty
Environmentalism

Debrief
Have the youth talk about their experience of the game and what it was like to talk about those hard things. See if there were any issues they wished the group had talked about. Take the time to talk about those.

Close in Prayer

Homework
Think about your big questions about God, reasons you struggle to believe in God, or any confusions you might have. Try to stump the Faith Diving leader with your odd and ridiculous questions!

Faith Diving Day 47
Big Questions
Location: Inside

Opening Prayer

Highs/Lows
Have the youth share a high event (good) and a low event (bad) from the last week.

Going Over The Homework
Ask the youth to get out their homework assignments. Ask them:
> What are your big questions about God, reasons you struggle to believe in God, or any confusions you have?
> Did you come up with any odd or ridiculous questions to stump your Faith Diving leader?

Big Questions
Hopefully they will come up with enough questions organically so that you don't have to make use of the below list, but try to prompt them to ask their own questions.

> What makes Christianity, Christianity? What is difficult about being a Christian?
> Is Baptism necessary? What about those who don't get Baptized?
> Is Communion really the body and blood of Jesus? Are you okay eating and drinking that?
> What's the hardest part of the Jesus story for you to believe?
> What about other religions/denominations? How do we know who is right?
> Heaven/Hell? Are they real? Who goes to Heaven? Who goes to Hell?
> Do you really have a Holy Spirit within you? Shouldn't you make the right decision more often?

How do we know we can trust what is in the Bible?
Can the Bible tell the future?
Is going to church really important?
Should we even have churches?
Shouldn't we just sleep in on Sundays and talk to God later?
What should churches be doing with their time?
Will you go to church when you or older?
Why do bad things happen to good people?
If God is so perfect, then why did God create something so imperfect allowing pain, suffering and daily atrocities?
How can someone be God's son and God at the same time?
Couldn't God have "saved" us another way than the cross?
Why doesn't God heal more people?
Why do some prayers seem to go unanswered?
Why doesn't God speak to us more clearly?
Why doesn't God just show himself to everyone at once so that everyone can believe?
If God created everything, why did God allow for AIDS, covid, cancer, and every other terrible thing?

Faith Letters

If confirmation day is approaching, talk to "graduating" youth about their faith letters. All the graduating Faith Divers are to write a letter to present on the Sunday of their graduation. Invite them to be open and honest about where their faith is at and where they think it is going.

Have them email these letters to you (the leader) to read and, no matter what, prompt them to say a little more and push them to be even more honest. They know what we want them to say, but we want to actually hear where they are.

Faith Diving, Confirmation Ritual
Explain to the graduating youth what sort of ritual your church uses for confirmation so they are prepared. Also, make sure to remind them that they are welcome to continue with faith diving.

For kids not graduating... two weeks after the graduation we will go see as "religious" a movie as we can find in theaters.

Close in Prayer

Homework
For the graduates, their homework is their faith letter. For the non-graduates encourage them to think about how we can learn about God, not just from religious things, but also from nearly anything... including a big box office movie that on the surface has almost nothing to do with God.

Faith Diving Day 48
Faith Diver Graduation
Location: Church

Faith Letter
All the Faith Divers are to write a letter to read in front of the church on the Sunday of their graduation. Invite them to be open and honest about where their faith is at and where they think it is going. At my church we have this faith diving sharing moment as the sermon for the day.

For youth who have a strong fear of speaking in public we have them record a video to share with the congregation.

Ritual
After the Faith Diver Faith Letter sharing time, hold whatever "Affirmation of Faith" ritual your church is accustomed to using.

End Year 3

Made in the USA
Monee, IL
21 September 2023